Telegram from
St. John's,

"Secret.
Naval Attache:
          LABEO
          PO
  BELLE ISLE
GROAIS
          ROUTE
PIG CRIER
ROBINEAU COVE
SIGNAL GRUN
SIGNAL ROTH
UXX one UNN

     This
submarines
course of
  have stated
at Miquelon
          Inform
          Address
Canada not

THE
SPRING RICE
DOCUMENT

Other Jack Fitzgerald books

Battlefront Newfoundland
Crimes That Shocked Newfoundland
Remarkable Stories of Newfoundland
The Jack Ford Story – Newfoundland's POW in Nagasaki
Legacy of Laughter
Newfoundland Adventures – In Air, On Land, At Sea
Ten Steps to the Gallows – True Stories of Newfoundland and Labrador
Treasure Island Revisited – A True Newfoundland Adventure Story
Newfoundland Disasters
Untold Stories of Newfoundland
Ghosts and Oddities
A Day at the Races – The Story of the St. John's Regatta
Beyond the Grave
Jack Fitzgerald's Notebook
Beyond Belief
The Hangman is Never Late
Another Time, Another Place
Where Angels Fear to Tread
Newfoundland Fireside Stories
Strange but True Newfoundland Stories
Amazing Newfoundland Stories
Up the Pond
Stroke of Champions
Too Many Parties, Too Many Pals
Convicted
Rogues and Branding Irons

Ask your favourite bookstore or order directly from the publisher.

Creative Book Publishing
430 Topsail Rd.,
St. John's, NL
A1E 4N1

Tel: (709) 748-0813
Fax: (709) 579-6511
E-mail: nl.books@transcontinental.ca
www.creativebookpublishing.ca

Telegram from ~~~~~
St. John's. ~~~~~

"Secret. ~~~~~
Naval Attache:

      LANGO ~~

      BO ~~~~

BELLE ISLE ~~~~
GROAIS ~~~~~~~~

    ROUTE ~~~

PIG~~~~~~~ ~~~ ~~
ROBINEAU COVE ~~

SIGNAL GRUN ~~~~~

SIGNAL ROTH ~~~~~

UXX one UX~ ~ ~~

    This ~~~~ ~~
submarines ~~~ ~~~
course of ~~~~~~~~

have stated t~ ~ ~
at Miquelon ~~~ ~~~

    Inform~~~ ~~

    Addressed ~~

Canada not ~~~~~~~~

THE
SPRING RICE
DOCUMENT
Newfoundland at War 1914-1918

Jack Fitzgerald

St. John's, Newfoundland and Labrador
2011

We gratefully acknowledge the financial support of the Canada Council for the Arts, the Government of Canada through the Canada Book Fund (CBF), and the Government of Newfoundland and Labrador through the Department of Tourism, Culture and Recreation for our publishing program.

Cover Design by Maurice Fitzgerald
Layout by Joanne Snook-Hann
Printed on acid-free paper

Published by
CREATIVE PUBLISHERS
an imprint of CREATIVE BOOK PUBLISHING
a Transcontinental Inc. associated company
P.O. Box 8660, Stn. A
St. John's, Newfoundland and Labrador A1B 3T7

Printed in Canada by:
TRANSCONTINENTAL INC.

Library and Archives Canada Cataloguing in Publication

Fitzgerald, Jack, 1945-
    The Spring Rice document : Newfoundland at war, 1914-1918 / Jack Fitzgerald.

Includes bibliographical references.
ISBN 978-1-897174-79-1

1. World War, 1914-1918--Newfoundland and Labrador. I. Title.

D547.N55F58 2011   940.3'718   C2011-905326-8

I dedicate
The Spring Rice Document, Newfoundland at War 1914-1918
to my niece Maureen her husband Gerry Peach
and their children, my grand-niece
Megan Peach and grand-nephew Ryan Peach.

ACKNOWLEDGEMENTS

I acknowledge with sincere appreciation the help of those who assisted me in my effort to bring *The Spring Rice Document* to publication. In particular, Bob Rumsey for his invaluable patience and dedicated editorial assistance, Maurice Fitzgerald for the cover design and photograph- editing, Don Morgan for the final manuscript editing and Donna Francis, of Creative Book Publishing for moral support and her work in tying up the loose ends prior to publication. I am also grateful for the professional work of Joanne Snook-Hann and Todd Manning, and Pam Dooley of Creative Book Publishing in the final preparations before going to press. Special thanks to Ken Byrne, Janine Lilly, Gwen Hansen, Owen Moore, and Mike Critch for their valuable encouragement and assistance; the staffs at the Provincial Archives of Newfoundland and Labrador, the Hunter Library (Newfoundland Collection), the Queen Elizabeth II Library, MUN, Centre of Newfoundland Studies, MUN and the City of St. John's Archives. I am grateful to Paul Sweeney and Stephen Sweeney for their time and effort in researching in the areas of Ayre, Glasgow and Edinburgh, Scotland.

TABLE OF CONTENTS

INTRODUCTION

Submarines during World War I were operable, not sophisticated. Other than sightings by fishermen off the Grand Banks and a boom put across the harbour in St. John's, the public's knowledge of the enemy's use of submarines around Newfoundland is limited. Not until Jack Fitzgerald's discovery of the "Spring Rice Document" between the pages of files he was using for his research at the Archives in St. John's, did he know how thoroughly Germany had investigated Newfoundland; how strategic it felt it was located, and what its plans were for its infiltration. Fitzgerald's find is crucial to our understanding of Newfoundland's overall involvement in the war.

The stories of the "Doomed Offences" as they are referred to by Winston Churchill are explored in detail in this book. The Battle of Gallipoli and the battles in France, to be specific, are presented realistically, and the reader is left armed to challenge traditional viewpoints.

This book leaves the reader with renewed pride in our Newfoundland Regiment, a force, at that time and in large measure, made up of volunteers with a background in the colony's cadet movement. These young men supplied the backbone of the famous "First Five Hundred" known as the "Blue Puttees". Newfoundland's contributions to the war were appreciated and admired by the peoples of the allied nations.

The extent of the Newfoundland Government's control of German aliens living in Newfoundland is noted and subjected to commentary. It is time that someone looked at the war with fresh eyes. This book gives new life to the story of Newfoundland's role in World War I.

Robert "Bob" Rumsey
Retired school teacher

Chapter 1

THE SPRING RICE DOCUMENT

What started in May 1915 as British Intelligence informing the Newfoundland Governor of "reliable rumours" that Germany was about to bring the war to the Northwest Atlantic caused heightened alarm in St. John's when, in July, the British obtained proof from an unexpected source. Details in a captured German document set off a chain of events in Newfoundland which had widespread repercussions.

The British Ambassador to Washington, Sir Cecil Spring Rice, had gotten access to German documents that fell into the hands of American officials after a major intelligence break occurred in New York on July 15, 1915. Among the captured papers were references to bays and coves in Newfoundland along with codes and the dates when U-boats would be in the areas. Because British Intelligence had already gathered information on Germany's intentions to launch an all-out submarine attack on British shipping in the northwest Atlantic, Spring Rice sent this particular item to the British Admiralty in London with a copy telegraphed to Captain G. Abraham, the British Intelligence Officer in St. John's.[1]

Captain G. H. Abraham, the British Intelligence Officer who shared the Spring Rice Document with the Newfoundland Government. (PANL)

At 6:40 p.m. on July 25th, just ten days after the intelligence break in the United States, Abraham received the alarming telegraph from the Ambassador. However, there was little detail on where or how the information was obtained, except to state that it was taken from the briefcase of a German Naval Attache. The

---

[1] Abraham appears to have been Britain's top intelligence agent in North America. The British Ambassador in Washington, shared the secret documents with Abraham before informing Canada. In fact, he left the responsibility of advising the Canadians to Abraham.

Telegram from British Ambassador, Washington, to I.O.
St. John's. Received 6.10 p.m. 25th July 1915.

"Secret. Following found amongst papers of German
Naval Attache:

          LANGO LANGENES 67 - 15.45

            BO GIMSC 68.47 - 14.60 U 81 89 94

  BELLE ISLE   55.20 - 52 UXX 3 RAD 11 60 3

GROAIS SISTERS 56.7 - 57 UXX 4 RAD 13 60 3

          ROUTE

PIGEONNIER ARM 7. 29-30

ROBINEAU COVE   9. 3-5

SIGNAL GRUN DUGGANS COVE 8 6-9

SIGNAL ROTH FOURCHETTE BAY 8 11-.

UXX one UXX 3 UXX 4 KLEIST DAM

   This seems to refer to routes, signals etc, of
submarines from July 29th to August 11th. In the
course of conversation German Naval Attache is said to
have stated that there are 3 men amongst fishermen
at Miquelon who were prepared to render assistance.
     Informant is a German Spy.
     Addressed to Foreign Office; sent to St. John's.
Canada not informed"

                         Spring Rice

The Spring Rice Document, was a top secret document with specific information concerning the times and places of German submarine arrivals in Newfoundland waters. These remained filed among Government records until discovered by author Jack Fitzgerald in 2010.

information obtained by Intelligence Officer Abraham was a very small part of widespread revelations that would have repercussions on the deteriorating relationship of the neutral United States with Germany. The captured documents were the property of Dr. Heinrich Albert, Naval Attache at the German Embassy in Washington and head of German propaganda in the United States.[2]

The ambassador's message to St. John's did not mention the shock waves the July 15th find was already sending through the top echelons of the American Government, military, and in particular, those who were fighting strongly to maintain America's neutrality. The sensational telegraph message said that the accompanying specific locations of several bays and coves in Newfoundland were found among the papers of a German Naval attache. Abraham, referring to the "Spring Rice Document" explained:

> It seems to refer to routes, signals etc. of submarines from July 29th to August 11th. In the course of conversation, the German Naval attache is said to have stated that there are three men among the fishermen at Miquelon preparing to render assistance to the plan.[3]

The communication was a copy of a page from the German records which mentioned the following locations in Newfoundland, and noted alongside each one was a series of numbers indicating the geographic location of: Belle Isle, Groais Sisters, Pigeonnier Arm, Robineau Cove, Duggan's Cove, etc. The Ambassador's message included the statement, "Informant is a German Spy. Addressed to Foreign Office; sent to St. John's. Canada not informed." The Intelligence Officer in St. John's was given approval from London to share the secret with the Canadian Ambassador to Washington. Less than one month later an assassination attempt was made on Sir Cecil Spring Rice when six men attacked his motor car as he was driving on a Washington Street. The attempt failed.[4]

---

[2] American intelligence conducted widespread investigation which included suspected spies and naval attache's at the German Embassy in Washington.
[3] PANL GN 1/3/A-Box 93.
[4] The Evening Telegram, September 3, page 7.

British Intelligence had already broken German Naval codes a year earlier.   On August 26, 1914, the German cruiser *Magdeburg* ran aground and was scuttled in the Gulf of Finland.   Several hours later, an Imperial Russian Navy ship entered the area and recovered the body of a German officer who was carrying top-secret documents including the German fleet's signal book.   The Russians handed over the documents to the British whose newly organized naval cryptanalysis centre succeeded in breaking the German code.[5]

Abraham also informed the Governor of an unconfirmed report that British Intelligence had received prior to the Spring-Rice Telegram which claimed that in mid-June four submarines had left Cuxhaven in the first week of June for the United States coast.   In addition, there were intelligence reports that two suspected enemy vessels sailing under a neutral flag had left American ports at the same time.   The British suspected that these ships were actually supply vessels for the submarines moving to the North Atlantic coastline.[6]

The source of this information may have been from an electronic advantage gained by the British on August 5, 1914.   On that date, the British cable ship *Teconia* raised the submarine cables off the German coast and cut them.   This action forced the Germans to reroute all their international communications through radio or another country's cables.   These passed through neutral territory and were easily monitored by the British for the rest of the war.[7]

British Intelligence Advises Newfoundland's Governor

Newfoundland was already preparing for a rumoured German offensive on North America.   Just days before Governor Davidson received the spy document he had been advised by British Intelligence on how the enemy could mount such an offensive.   Now, armed with the Spring Rice Document, that advice from the British took on an immediate priority.   Captain G. Abraham had explained to Davidson:

---

[5] H. Robert Ferrell, general editor, <u>The Twentieth Century, An Almanac</u>.
[6] Ibid.
[7] David Miller, <u>U-Boats, History, Development and Equipment 1914-1945</u>.

If it is the enemy's intention to send submarines across the Atlantic to attack British ships, arrangements have doubtless been made to secure means of communicating with many agents both here and on the coast of the Dominion and the United States. Their plans would understandably be completed, not only for the arrangement of bases of supply, but also for information as to the movement of British ships of war and merchant vessels.

It may pay the Germans to send one or two large and modern submarines to intercept the summer traffic through the Bell Isle Straits, but I am convinced they will only be sent in company with supply ships fitted out in Europe and disguised as foreign trawlers. Assuming that a harbour has been selected suitable for the purpose, it will not, I think, be on the Newfoundland coast. The submarine must come by a very northerly route, via the Norwegian and Iceland coasts, and would therefore seek a northerly base for receiving supplies.

Their plan therefore would be to wait until The Strait of Belle Isles are open to traffic and base their plans for attacking the line of traffic debouching from the Straits at some point out of sight of shore but no more than one hundred or two hundred miles from their base on Labrador.[8]

The Labrador area of the colony was of special importance to British Intelligence. Abraham explained:

We are concerned that if the German's set up a Labrador base they could take control of a telegraph office for their own purposes and we might not know. The telegraph stations will remain open as usual. Each operator would be required to send on a daily basis a code word that would be changed weekly.[9]

---

[8] PANL 1/3/A.
[9] Ibid.

After presenting his view on what German strategy would be, Abraham advised Davidson that Newfoundland's first move should be to seek Canada's cooperation in closing The Strait of Belle Isle to ships from Europe for the summer of 1915. He said this could easily be done in conjunction with the guarding of the route through the Cabot Strait. The Intelligence Officer felt that the German submarines may never receive the information that traffic was diverted from The Strait of Belle Isle[10], especially if they miss the usual notice in telegraphs to Lloyds of London and an announcement in the American newspapers that The Strait of Belle Isle are now, as usual, open for traffic. When this suggestion was discussed with Canada, the Canadians disagreed with closing the straits but agreed to accept the responsibility to patrol them.

Captain Abraham, just days before, had discussed other steps the enemy would have to take to follow through on its intention to send submarines to the northwest Atlantic. Abraham explained that bases of supply would be needed to service the enemy fleet and these would likely be set up, "...in out of the way bays of Newfoundland, Labrador or off St. Pierre."

The Intelligence Officer pointed out that part of Newfoundland's response effort needed to include a country wide monitoring of supplies, particularly those needed to support submarines (i.e. oils, lubricating oils, hardware supplies, unusually high orders of food, water, medicines etc).

Upon the advice of Captain Abraham, Newfoundland customs officers were ordered to gather information from all British and neutral ships coming into Newfoundland regarding any sightings and locations of vessels acting suspiciously. They were told to report immediately any such information gathered to government authorities. All British vessels were supplied with listings of local authorities to whom such information had to be reported. Newfoundland also agreed to create a system of land patrols and patrols by small vessels to watch the coast for suspicious activity.

The Spring Rice Document, despite its widespread consequences, was never made public in Newfoundland and remained a secret. It did, however, prompt the government to immediately intensify its approach to censorship and the treatment of enemy aliens.

---

[10] The Belle Isle Straits is commonly known as The Strait of Belle Isle.

The cloak and dagger episode began on July 1915, with the finding of a briefcase which was left on a New York subway, and ended up in the hands of American Intelligence. Inside the briefcase were secret German documents revealing an extensive network of espionage and subversion across the United States.[11] On August 15, 1915, the *New York World* began publishing details of the espionage story which were given to them by the U.S. Secretary of the Treasury, William G. McAdoo.

The British Ambassador's message to the Intelligence Officer in St. John's was a single sheet of written information relating to Newfoundland which had been recovered from the captured spy files. Following an almost six month investigation by the Americans, it was concluded that military and naval attaches were involved in the elaborate spying and espionage program. On December 1, 1915, the United States demanded that Germany withdraw its military and naval attaches from the Washington Embassy.[12]

The Plan to Thwart German Infiltration

The captured German document indicated the area of concentration for the German plan in Newfoundland was in The Strait of Belle Isle and the Harbour Deep area of the Northern Peninsula. A week after learning of the plan, the Government's response strategy went into action. Two armed patrol boats each carrying armed members of the Newfoundland Regiment were on their way to set up military stations in coves identified in the document.[13]

Lieutenant Norris and Lieutenant O'Grady, each in command of forty non-commissioned-officers of the Newfoundland Regiment, left St. John's by train for Lewisporte where they boarded the S.S *Home* to begin their secret mission. Their assignment was to guard the places referenced in the spy document which were in the White Bay area: Pigeonnier Arm, Great Harbour Deep and Duggan's Cove situated outside its entrance. Fourchette Bay and Robinson Cove which are located

---

[11] H. Robert Ferrell, editor, <u>Twentieth Century Almanac</u>.
[12] Ibid.
[13] Plans to outfit several patrol boats for Northern Newfoundland were in progress at the time the "Spring Rice Document" was sent to Newfoundland. Now, armed with specific information, the Government stepped up its plans.

near the entrance to Harbour Deep were also guarded. The soldiers were armed only with rifles only and were ordered to capture any supply ships which reached these rendezvous points and to keep the Governor informed daily by telegraph. Governor Davidson felt Lieutenant Norris was ideal for the assignment because his father was the leading merchant in Green Bay and White Bay, and his brother was the manager of an agency in Conche.

Around the same time, a second patrol vessel rushed to the area of Groais Islands. This was the SS *Petrel* with the Hon. A. W. Piccott, Minister of Marine, in charge and Lieutenant Commander A. MacDermott, RN, in military command. A third vessel the SS *Fogota* transported another forty member detachment of the Newfoundland Regiment to join MacDermott's party and to occupy the Groais Islands. The SS *Petrel* also carried an experienced Royal Navy Reserve gun crew who were trained to handle the two eight-pounder guns on board. The Marconi Telegraph Company sent an engineer to install a wireless telegraph system on the patrol boat.

Newfoundland entered into an agreement with the Canadian Government for the Canadian Navy to patrol The Strait of Belle Isle. The SS *Hump* from Newfoundland was already on patrol and operating from a station in Northern Labrador with headquarters in Nain which had a wireless connection with the Canadian system in Belle Isle and Point Riche.

Captain Abraham Recommended Alien Arrests

Captain Abraham, in a confidential document sent to Governor Davidson, urged that he act immediately to arrest all enemy subjects in Newfoundland and Labrador who were still at large, as well as, deport all those, "...who actively sympathise with the enemy."

Just days before receiving the Spring Rice Document, Abraham told Davidson:

> Should enemy submarines come to this part of the world, it is to be expected that they will have arranged for several bases or places in which to meet their supply ships on various points of the coast, partly for safety and partly to increase their range of action. It would be of value to them

to have their agents in various places, especially if the latter could supply them with information concerning our precautionary measures. These duties could be performed by enemy subjects in this country or those who sympathise with the enemy. They could communicate their information to the United States in some 'en clair code'[14] without arousing suspicion, whence it could reach the enemy.[15]

Davidson, armed with specific locations and dates on which submarines were expected to be in Newfoundland waters, became more resolved in his response actions.

Repercussions of the Spring Rice Document spread

In view of the Spring Rice Document the Newfoundland Governor was forced to have a further look at the presence of the Moravian German missionaries in Labrador. There were fifteen members of the Labrador mission, nine of whom were German subjects and six were British. He communicated his views to the Colonial Secretary in London, Bonar Law:

The Newfoundland Government recommends that authority be given to the Justice of the Peace officers now on duty in Labrador to arrest eight of these enemy aliens and to bring them to St. John's for the purpose of internment for the period of the war. I would advise that Bishop Martine at Nain should be permitted to stay, in view of his age and of his long residence on the coast, and remain in executive charge of the mission work. He would still have help of six persons, either the missionary or storekeepers and the only doctor to look after the affairs of the mission.

I express this opinion after much deliberation, not so much because I suspect their hostile intent nor believe in their power to do mischief, but because the coast in their charge is likely to be made use of as a submarine base and

---

[14] The Oxford Dictionary defines 'en clair code' as a code in ordinary language.
[15] PANL G1/100 reel #2 document #295. Letter from G.E.F. Abraham.

because they cannot be expected to denounce their compatriots.[16]

The Newfoundland Governor's resolve to deal with the pending crisis is reflected in the following message he sent to the Governor General of Canada:

We should undoubtedly and justifiably be open to censure if, despite the official warning we have received, we should still permit to be at large enemy subjects and others who have openly shown their sympathy with the enemy. Moreover, apart from the anxiety and the responsibility, the Government is also put to considerable expense to guard the shores and to watch the actions of possible enemy agents. For instance, the cost of putting in commission the *Hump* as a patrol vessel is a strict outcome of our knowledge that a number of enemy subjects are at large in settlements on the coast of Labrador and then from evidence before us, not I admit of the best quality, that certain of these enemy subjects have expressed views which are not in sympathy with our cause.[17]

Although the government initiated a policy dealing with enemy aliens and censorship when the war broke out, a new intensified policy emerged as a consequence of the Spring Rice papers.

The Governor sought and received approval from Britain to the impose the following policy regarding aliens. In respect to this condition, Governor Davidson in a message to Hon. A. Bonar Law, a member of the British War Cabinet, made the following recommendations:

All enemy subjects not already in custody should 'now' be picked up and interred. I should advise that an exception be made in favour of enemy aliens of German nationality by birth, who can prove continual residence on the American continent for the last twenty years. Enemy aliens already interred be prevented from transmitting messages

---

[16] PANL GN 1/3 Box 93.
[17] PANL GN 1/3/A.

through third parties or other enemy subjects. As regards to persons who not being of enemy nationality can be shown to be actively in sympathy with the enemy. I know of only one person who fails in this category, namely, Mr. Rockwell Kent, a subject of the United States at present residing in Brigus. In the case of this man there is ample evidence, officially on record, to show that he is hostile in intention and I should advise that he be required to leave the colony on the first opportunity.[18]

Huesbsch

L. Huesbsch was a naturalised American subject, but, by birth, an enemy alien. At a time when British Intelligence was expecting German submarines to seek out- of- the way coves and bays along the Labrador coast as bases to attack Allied interests on the Atlantic, he sought to do business in Labrador.

He was planning to travel throughout Labrador purchasing furs for a firm to be marketed in enemy territory believed to be German owned. Newfoundland authorities had already been warned about the likelihood of suspicious visitors in Labrador scouting out the coast for the enemy while operating under the guise of doing legitimate business.

When the matter was referred to Newfoundland's Justice Department, Huesbsch was advised to return to the United States. The deputy minister of justice pointed out, "The export of furs of which the ultimate destination may be enemy territory has been prohibited by Order in Council, furs being conditional contraband." The Governor was concerned over the possibility of foreigners on business communicating intelligence to the enemy through their business contacts.

James S. Hansen, another visiting businessman who was already travelling in Labrador buying furs, was deported at the same time and for similar reasons.

First POW Camps in Newfoundland

The legal basis for proceeding against enemy aliens in Newfoundland became the War Measures Act passed by the

---

[18] Ibid.

Newfoundland Legislature on September 7, 1914, and was made retroactive to August 1st. This legislation was modelled on similar legislation passed by the Canadian and British Parliaments. The act provided Government with, "... wide discretionary powers to arrest, detain, and to deport undesirables in the interest of "the security, defence, peace order and welfare of Newfoundland[19]."

On August 19, 1914, His Majesty's Penitentiary (HMP) located on Forest Road in St. John's became the first designated POW camp in Newfoundland. Those POWs held at HMP complained about being treated as criminals, the lack of recreation, and poor quality of food. The Governor of the Penitentiary responded to this criticism:

> It is the best scale of dietary known here. Namely: tea, porridge, molasses and biscuit every morning. Fish and potatoes, biscuit, and tea for dinner on Mondays, Wednesdays and Friday. Pea Soup and biscuit on Saturdays. Fresh meat, rice, soup and biscuit on Tuesday, Thursdays and Saturdays. – July 19, 1915.[20]

Soon after this episode, the POWs were moved to other facilities in Harbour Grace, Placentia and the Bay of Islands. As a consequence of the Spring Rice Document, the Government leased a premises on Topsail Road, known as Donovans, located about seven miles west of St. John's which they converted into a detention camp for POWs. These prisoners were eventually transferred to the Donovans "concentration camp."

Prior to this the camp was being used for military convalescents and had an observatory. This gave the patients an excellent view of the country area. The Newfoundland Regiment considered it too far out of town for them to use.[21]

During WWII the Royal Canadian Navy used the facility as a rest and relaxation camp for sailors who had spent longer than normal periods at sea. It had a large cookhouse, three quantum huts, a large outdoor swimming pool constructed on a stream, and a large cabin for officers. In 1946, the Kinsmen Club of St. John's

---

[19] Ibid.
[20] PANL GN/1/100 reel #2.
[21] Ibid.

took over the property and used it as a boys' summer camp. In 1952, four wooden bunk houses were added to the three Quonset huts. The wartime officers cabin housed the camp counsellors and included a canteen.[22] The famous Newfoundland singer, Biddy O'Tool lived in a small white house next to the property.[23] Today, the site is occupied by Sears of Canada.

London ordered Internment of Aliens

Within days of War being declared, British Secretary of State, Bonar Law, instructed the Newfoundland Government to arrest and detain all German military reservists regardless if they were serving on British or neutral ships. The rationale behind the move was to provide Britain with leverage in dealing with the Germans over the treatment of captured British and allied soldiers and officers. The round up of these men, described as "enemy aliens" began almost immediately as did the internment of Newfoundland citizens of German origins.

The fears that Germany would bring the war to the shores of Newfoundland were widespread from the start of the conflict and intensified as the war progressed. In December 1914, the *Montreal Star* published a news item that caught Newfoundlanders' attention. The article raised the issue of German spies operating in Newfoundland asked, "How far is St. John's used as a spy centre?"

The story was based on reported claims by the manager of the Nova Scotia Steel Company, owners of the Bell Island Mines, that the German arms dealer Krupp was in possession of the most detailed information about the Bell Island Mining Operation. Germany was one of the mine's biggest customers before the war. The article suggested that the information could be used by the enemy in any plans to attack or invade Canada.

During this period when anti-German sentiments in Newfoundland was growing, a rather startling incident occurred. A man who had been dead for two months, and who was a long

---

[22] It is not clear whether the officer's cabin was the original from WWI or one built or renovated in WWII by the Royal Canadian Navy.

[23] Biddy O'Tool, a member of the Uncle Tim's Barn Dance Troupe, is best remembered for the song, "I met her in the garden where the praties grow," which she sang on stage at the Knights of Columbus in St. John's on December 12, 1942 when it was destroyed by fire and ninety-nine people lost their lives. See Newfoundland Disasters, Jack Fitzgerald.

time active and respected member of the community, Robert von Stein, was accused of carrying out under-cover work for Germany.

Dead Citizen accused of Spying

Robert von Stein, an engineer whose professional work was evident in St. John's and as far from the city as Salmonier Line, where he constructed bridges, was also famous for his work with the St. John's Regatta Committee. He served on the executive of that committee for years and introduced many novel attractions to lakeside for the enjoyment of the general public.

The basis for the accusation was a report in the St. John's *Mail and Advocate* on September 12, 1914, which claimed that the *North Sydney Herald* had conclusive proof from private reliable sources of Stein's systematic gathering of intelligence for the Kaiser. One of Von Stein's sons, Conrad, enlisted in the Newfoundland Regiment and served in the 3rd Battalion.

Stein's sister-in-law publicly defended him and denied that there was any basis to the article which she said was nothing but "slander."

Mike Critch one of the most recognizable voices from radio station VOCM's long history. Critch is nephew of Peter Kercher who was suspected of being a German spy during WWI. Kercher was rounded up with other German aliens and imprisoned at the Donovan's Concentration Camp seven miles from St. John's. There was no evidence that Kercher was a spy, but he was deported from Newfoundland in 1915.
(Courtesy Mike Critch)

Suspected German Spy owned Escasoni Property

Mike Critch, an icon of Newfoundland radio history, has an interesting family connection with one of the intriguing spy stories of World War I. An uncle of Critch's, Peter Kercher, was arrested as a "German spy suspect" in St. John's soon after the breakout of WWI and allowed to leave Newfoundland in the aftermath of the Spring Rice Document under certain restrictions.

In the fall of 1914, Kercher, then thirty-five years old and a steward on the S.S *Florizel*, was dismissed from his job as the result of the Government's

Peter Kercher, a German immigrant to Newfoundland, was suspected of spying for Germany during WWI. In 1915, he was held at the Donovan's POW Camp on Topsail Road. He is shown in this photograph taken in a Brooklyn, New York photo studio with his Newfoundland born wife Alice Critch. (Courtesy of Mike Critch)

enemy alien policy. It was a time when German aliens in Newfoundland were being rounded up, and the public was alarmed by daily news reports and speculation of German activities off the Newfoundland coast. They feared that the colony itself might come under attack. Many respectable Newfoundland citizens with German origins who before the war were highly esteemed and treated as fellow countrymen were being shunned by friends.[24]

Kercher had been a resident of Newfoundland for ten years before being accused, and had spent his childhood in the United States. While searching for the maiden name of Mrs. Peter Kercher, I learned of Mike Critch's connection to the Kerchers. In discussing the story with Critch, he commented, "Finding Peter's wife's name is not too difficult, it was Alice Critch, my aunt Alice. As a matter of fact I still have a picture of Peter and Alice taken at a photo studio in Brooklyn, New York."

Kercher was kept at the Donovan's POW camp on Topsail Road. Authorities who got to know him were most impressed by his exemplary character and his outstanding performance of work assignments. Kercher was a major influence in helping to maintain discipline and order in the camp.

His performance at Donovan's played a role in his not being sent to the Canadian POW camps when others were moved there. Instead, he was set free with the conditions that he move to the United States, pay a $4000 bond to stay there and report twice a month to the British Consular Agent in New York. Although his British naturalization papers were forfeited, these were returned to him after the war.[25]

---

[24] PANL GN2-14 Box 13, file 152.
[25] Ibid.

Peter Kercher became an American citizen in 1907, and in August 1914 became a British subject. He was arrested and interned in July 1915, but he was excluded from other arrested German aliens when they were deported for imprisonment in Canadian POW camps. His arrest, and the arrest of others, was part of Newfoundland's policy towards aliens during WWI.

Mike Critch never met his uncle, but did know his Aunt Alice who lived to be 100 years old. When the epidemic of Spanish Flu was sweeping the world in 1918, and there was an urgent need for hospital space in St. John's for sick and injured veterans returning from Europe, the Government looked to the fifty acre property on Portugal Cove Road called Escasoni.[26] Once authorities moved to rent or purchase it, they discovered it was owned by Peter Kercher, the German they had declared as an enemy alien. The Governor pointed out that because of wartime legislation relating to trading with the enemy he could not deal with Kercher. However, they did take control of the Escasoni property, and turned it into a sanatorium for the troops.[27] It was an ideal spot for a hospital and in 1918 was well outside St. John's and was surrounded by farms, grassy fields and nearby rivers.

Mike Critch recalled that Escasoni housed a very large residence and there was a second building on the property. He remembered having outings there many years later when the buildings had been vacated and were deteriorating. Mike said that one of the most impressive features of Escasoni was the outside balcony that surrounded the house. He reminisced about old family photos, long disappeared, showing patients sitting outside on the balcony when it was being used as a soldier's hospital. Critch said that when Peter was not using it himself, his uncle rented it out.

Some years later when Kercher passed away, he left in his will, property and money in St. John's to a Newfoundland family he had befriended while living in the colony. Mike recalled that his aunt and uncle settled down in New Jersey and his aunt kept in touch with relatives in St. John's by letters, but as time passed, they heard less and less from her. Mike Critch was awarded the Radio–

---

[26] The prominent Emerson family later obtained the property which continued to be called Escasoni.
[27] PANL GN-214 Box 13 File 141.

Television News Director's Association of Canada's *Lifetime Achievement Award* in 2008.

Warschauer

Richard Warschauer, a German businessman, moved to St. John's early in 1914 and was manager of the Newfoundland Trading Company of New York. Soon after, he married a Newfoundland girl. His main business was the buying of tinned lobsters for the firm of Rosenstein & Company, New York. This work required him to travel to the outports of the colony regularly and he became familiar with most places. Warschauer fitted the profile of an enemy operator in Newfoundland as described by Captain Abraham.

The British had supplied Newfoundland censors with lengthy lists of firms and people outside Newfoundland which were suspected of having German connections. This reference source was a major tool of the Chief Censor's office. It was this listing that led to the two arrests of Warschauer.

Like Kercher, Warschauer was considered an enemy alien and was automatically brought under the scrutiny of the chief censor. When they noted that he was sending frequent mail to a company in Philadelphia on their index listings, he was arrested and imprisoned, but not for long. Several prominent citizens vouched for him, and he was released on $4000 bail. While in prison, Warschauer was suspected of smuggling mail to the outside. His explanation for the actual mail, which was of concern to the censors, was that he was trying to collect bad debts from the Philadelphia company. His lawyer were A. B. Morine, K.C., M.H.A., and a prominent member of the Newfoundland Patriotic Association.

The suspected spy was not free for long. Once he was released from HMP, he was placed under police surveillance. The amount of mail he had been sending to the United States dropped significantly which led censors to suspect he was circumventing the censorship laws by using a third party to get mail outside the country.[28] At this time Davidson advised the Justice Department, "It is especially important at this juncture to have the strictest guard on him and his communications." Specifically referring to the Spring Rice Document, Davidson said, "In view of renewed

---

[28] PANL GN-2-14 Box 3.

enemy threats of hostility, it is necessary to make Warschauer absolutely secure, and I advise his being again remanded to the Penitentiary."

His bail bonds were forfeited, and he was again arrested and held as a prisoner of war. The prisoner was told that prosecution was possible under the "Defence of the Realm Legislation." The fact that he was an officer in the German Reserve was an added factor in his becoming a POW. The accused was a German subject and of military age. In an interview with Governor Davidson, Warschauer admitted he had qualified to be enrolled as a German Reserve Officer and if he was in Germany he would serve in the German Army. When on bail, he stayed at O'Rorke's Hotel in Holyrood not far from St. John's. The prisoner did not face prosecution and after a short while at Donovan's POW Camp, he was sent to an internment camp in Canada.

Two days after he received the Spring Rice Document, Governor Davidson requested that the POWs in the outport jails be transferred to the Donovan's concentration camp which was guarded by thirty armed soldiers from the Newfoundland Regiment. The POW camp housed twenty prisoners.

Sometimes allegations of German spying led police to a dead end, as was the following case which made the newspapers.

A foreign speaking man arriving in St. John's from Bell Island on Saturday, July 8, 1916, caused excitement among city people over rumours that he was a German spy. The incident attracted the attention of the Newfoundland Constabulary.

The *Evening Telegram* reported:

> He registered at a certain boarding house as a Russian. By a curious coincidence, it happened that two other men of that nationality were staying there. However, all three became very friendly and started to converse. At the outset, one of the genuine Russians, having a fair knowledge of the German language, discovered that the newcomer knew nothing about the Russian tongue, as professed, but on the contrary, was found to be a versatile German, judging by his talk.

The Russians were in St. John's to purchase two Newfoundland ships for Russia. After the Russian notified the Constabulary, the mystery guest disappeared. The newspaper suggested he had been, "... aided and abetted by a foreign businessman whose proclivities are known not to be at all in sympathy with the flag under which he lives."

Rockwell Kent

The Spring Rice Document had a direct affect on the firm position taken by the Newfoundland Governor regarding Rockwell Kent. Kent, a world famous artist, was deported from his home in Brigus, Conception Bay days after British Intelligence passed the captured papers to the Governor. As previously mentioned, the Governor's letter to the Colonial Secretary stated he was concerned over public suspicions that Kent was a German spy might lead to mob violence.

Kent, a winner of the Lenin Peace Prize, chose to settle in Brigus because of its natural beauty and the much easier pace of living compared to the rest of North America. In February 1914, he rented a Victorian style house there which required some upgrading. Kent carried out the repairs himself and then sent for his wife and three daughters in the United States. Most people of Brigus welcomed Kent and family as neighbours but were indifferent to his work as an artist. Others viewed him with suspicion which intensified once war broke out.

The daily news of the events taking place in Europe and North America inspired a general suspicion of all foreigners, and especially naturalized aliens. When police began rounding up German aliens for questioning, it did not take long before the people of Brigus were pointing a finger at Kent. The artist did little to help his situation. He displayed an attitude of contempt towards the people of Brigus by trivializing their wartime fears of Germans. He not only mocked them but also mocked the police sent to Brigus to enforce the actions undertaken by the Justice Department in accordance with the Wartime Measures Act.

The first rumour spread about the artist was that he was a German spy, and kept his art studio under lock and key because he was using it to draw geographic maps of Newfoundland for the enemy.

In reality, there was no need for concern because the artist's studio work had nothing to do with German espionage but contained artwork to be sent to an agent in New York to sell. In

April 1915, his New York agent, George S. Chappell, 101 Park Avenue, New York City, found a buyer for a collection of Rockwell's drawings. When he requested directions from Kent, the artist sent the following telegraph: "Sell drawings on condition that you appropriate six for self. This is a magnificent stroke of business. I am delighted and grateful to you"[29]

It appears, because of the growing suspicions of him among the Brigus population, that when he found it necessary to go to Boston in May 1915 on undisclosed legal business, he arranged for his family to stay at 6 King's Road in St. John's. From Boston on May 17th, Rockwell Kent sent the following telegraph to his wife:

Preliminary hearing Friday. Everything proceeding satisfactorily. There will be plenty of excitement though. I am confident of the outcome. Good lawyers are acting for me. Very lonely. Tried to hire flute but couldn't. Write to me right away and wire if anything occurs eager to hear from you.[30]

All telegraphs and letters to and from Rockwell Kent were being stopped and screened by censors before delivery. The above telegraph was referred to the Deputy Chief Censor and then released.

The next aspect of Kent's life that attracted the attention of neighbours was the large tool chest he kept on his property. They suggested he was using it to store bombs or the tools to make one.

When Kent stored seven tons of coal for the coming winter another suspicion of him spying was added to those already circulating. "He must be storing the coal as fuel for German U-boats operating on the Atlantic," they said. Then an incident occurred at a school concert that convinced some people that Rockwell Kent was indeed a German spy. Kent participated in the concert by singing German songs. Kent, who was not at all German, had remembered some favourite German songs from his youth which he performed at several Brigus concerts.[31]

---

[29] PANL GN 2-14 Box 3.
[30] Ibid.
[31] Dr. Gerhard Bassler, From Vikings to U-boats.

Meanwhile, Kent had heard all the rumours and was amused by them. He did have his supporters in the community. A dozen or so Brigus residents were genuine and loyal friends and gave no heed to the stories. Kent, however, found it amusing to joke about the situation. He painted a yellow sign on his front door that read, "Bomb Shelter, Chart Room, Wireless Station." Beneath the sign he drew a German Eagle.

The rumours spread outside the community and reached police offices in St. John's. The Inspector General of Police, Charles Hutchings, was already coping with daily allegations from all over the colony about German aliens and other foreigners and each one got police attention. As in each such allegation, a police officer was sent to inform a suspect of the allegations and, in this case, Kent was invited to go to St. John's for a meeting with the Inspector General of Police.

Kent's actions continued to draw the attention of his opponents in Brigus and Newfoundland authorities. He wrote his friends in German, knowing it would be viewed by the censors, and he even expressed in the writings a wish for German victory in the war.

Then a statement made by Kent on May 22, 1915, in the *New Republic* sealed his fate in Newfoundland. In the article he denounced Britain and cursed Newfoundland. This came at a time when Newfoundlanders were dealing with news of family members dying on the battlefields of Europe.

Sir Richard Squires investigated Kent's background and gathered information from American authorities concluded that Kent was no spy and no threat to Newfoundland. This was a view shared by Governor Davidson. Their main concern was that the hysteria developing over the issue could lead to more serious problems and threaten the safety Kent's family.

Brigus Leaders Support Kent

Some of the leading citizens of Brigus came to Rockwell Kent's defence. There were nine of them: S.W. Bartlett, William Bartlett, J. W. Hiscock, Dr. J. N. McDonald, S. E. Chafe, J. C. Cozens, R. E. Maddock, John Smith, Justice of Peace and T. C. Makinson. They submitted a letter to the Inspector General of Police who sent a copy to the Governor.

The group recognized that Kent created problems for himself, but they explained that he was an intelligent and accomplished individual whose ordinary demeanor was to speak frankly without fear. They noted that Kent had a "strong liking" for the German people. This, they said, was not unusual for an American college-bred man who spent some time as a student in Germany.

The letter stated:

> It is highly improbable that Mr. Kent as a socialist, has any particular regard for the Kaiser or the military aristocracy of Germany. The spread of socialism is Mr. Kent's desire, not the aggrandizement of the most bitter opponents of socialism in the world.
>
> We shall be sorry to be deprived of all opportunity to hold further conversations with Mr. Kent, and can assure him that there are Newfoundlanders who do not regard him with suspicion and dislike.

The petition of his supporters and the intervention of the American Consul in St. John's were to no avail, and in July 1915, the order for Rockwell Kent's deportation was issued. Governor Davidson himself did not believe that Kent was an enemy agent and felt that the decision to expel him from the country would have been deferred had it not been for the German threats revealed in the Spring Rice Document. Davidson said:

> It had become necessary, out of consideration of public safety to intern enemy subjects of military age and to exercise surveillance over others who openly expressed their sympathy with the King's enemies. Mr. Kent concurs in the reasonableness of this decision and has undertaken in response to this invitation to leave the country.[32]

A week later, Kent asked the Governor to grant him a one month extension to his deadline to leave due to sickness in his family and the time needed to prepare for the move. The

---

[32] PANL GN 1/100 reel #2.

Governor approved the request because he believed Rockwell Kent was not in the employ of the enemy nor in direct correspondence with known enemy agents.

Kent's Private Telegraphs

Among the Colonial Secretary's files at the Rooms are several of the intercepted telegraphs to, or from, Rockwell Kent during WWI. Kent sent the following telegraph to Mrs. Kent in Tarrytown, New York, July 19th:

> Letter arrived today. We expected you. Children in tears all upset. You must come. Will make any sacrifices and will return most remittance immediately. Daniel will assist. Visit worth any amount to K [Kathleen]. We have prepared for weeks. Come Red Cross. Best way start now.[33]

Somehow, this message escaped censors and was sent directly which caused John R. Bennett, Deputy Chief Censor, to write to American Telegraph:

> I must express my surprise that you have passed this message, for it should certainly have been held up. You have in the past referred all these messages to this office, and this practice should have been adhered to in the present case.[34]

He asked that "all" letters and telegraphs to Rockwell Kent be first sent to the censor's office.

On July 20th, Kent, who had been expecting his wife to return from the United States, sent the following telegraph to her in Tarrytown, New York:

> Don't come. We have decided, all come see you and stay. Don't know just how dispose ourselves on arrival but will find way. Kathleen delighted at decision. Best way to

---

[33] PANL GN2-14 Box 3. Colonial Secretary's Files.
[34] Ibid.

spend the money which I hope you have sent. Have written particulars all well and eager to return to civilization.[35]

Kent was escorted to the St. John's Harbour where police made sure he left the country. On August 7, 1915, he sent the following message from New London, Connecticut, to Bessie Noseworthy in Brigus:

We are settled in New London, Connecticut, and want you with us, as soon as you can get here. Come to the next Florizel and bring Marcy if you want to. I have written sending money. Don't fail us. I will meet you in New York from Halifax.- Rockwell Kent.[36]

That appears to be the last of the unfortunate Rockwell Kent episode in Newfoundland but not the last of Kent. His reputation and stature in the arts spread worldwide. In 1968, Premier Joseph R. Smallwood acknowledged that a wrong had been done to Rockwell Kent and his family and extended an invitation to Kent and his wife to visit Newfoundland. Kent agreed and a banquet was held in his honour at Memorial University in July 1968.

Kent was impressed with how Newfoundland had progressed since he left it and told Smallwood, "Why not let us have you on lend-lease for awhile? My God, how we and all mankind need men like you today."

Controlling Secret Information

A picture of a British submarine in St. John's Harbour published in the August 5, 1915 issue of the *New York Times* caused alarm at the British Admiralty offices in London and set off a major police investigation in St. John's.

To deal with the threat of German cruisers to troop movements and shipping off the Newfoundland and Canadian coasts, the British Admiralty had sent several submarines to these areas of the North Atlantic. Their purpose, presence, and location were military secrets and the job of censors was to make sure that

---

[35] Ibid.
[36] Ibid.

any mention of them that would aid the enemy was kept out of the press.

In response to this breach of censorship, the Admiralty sent a stern message to the Colonial Secretary in Newfoundland with instructions to find the Janet Cummings who sold the picture and to make sure that she, and others concerned, were aware of the censorship laws. The Colonial Secretary called upon the Inspector General of Police to launch an immediate investigation. Hutchings was also asked to conduct a citywide search of the businesses in the city, especially photography outlets, to make sure that military pictures were passed over to the censors for a decision on whether or not they could be sold.

The police investigation found photographers and shops that were selling photographs of military personnel and Naval vessels visiting St. John's Harbour and gave them warnings. R.P Holloway, owner of Holloway's Studio, a major city photography outlet, asked the Colonial Secretary to clarify the censorship laws. He wrote:

> This is a far-reaching order. Should we discontinue sale of such pictures as: groups of naval reserves, regional groups, and sailors on board ships in the harbour? Does it apply to all new pictures, or only to late ones, or the oldest which have already been in the foreign newspapers?[37]

The Colonial Secretary, Hon. John Bennett, responded to Holloway's concerns:

> In general terms, the idea is that no pictures shall be circulated which shall, in any way, aid the enemy or give information of any measures being taken for his circumvention. A strict definition is not possible, and the obvious course is to err on the safe side.[38]

Bennett also told Holloway that for the time being the restrictions are only on submarine movements in St. John's Harbour and pictures and post cards of this nature were not to be sold at all.

---

[37] PANL GN 2-14 File 8.
[38] Ibid.

In respect to pictures of troops leaving, these were not to be released until the troops had arrived safely at their destinations. Earlier in the year, on May 22nd, when the *Daily News* published that troops were leaving on the *Calgarian*, all newspapers were held at the post office until the safe arrival of the troops in England was confirmed. Governor Davidson reminded the press:

> The organization by the enemy for collecting news from this side of the Atlantic is elaborate; any indication of dates for the transit of troops will certainly be transmitted to Germany. We must disclose nothing which may risk the lives of our men in their voyage across the ocean.[39]

Holloway assured Mr. Bennett and Mr. Hutchings of his full cooperation. Soon after, he submitted several pictures of a military nature to the censor which he had hoped to sell to the *Daily Star* but was turned down. Parsons, the second major photography studio in St. John's, was also visited by police and given similar warnings to those passed on to Holloway. The Colonial Secretary then offered to compensate photographers for their losses.

However, when the *Newfoundland Quarterly* published censored pictures in October, while local photographers were prevented from selling theirs, Holloway complained. Bennett contacted Holloway and explained that the *Newfoundland Quarterly* material had been prepared and gone to the press before censorship rules were published.

As a result of the dispute with Holloway, the Colonial Secretary ordered all those with plans to publish Christmas issues to submit pictures relating to His Majesty's military forces, ships or any sort of military connection to the censor's office. A public notice regarding the censorship of the press was issued on October 15, 1915, under the provisions of the War Measures Act of 1914.

A prominent journalist of that era, Patrick T. McGrath, attracted the attention of censors during July 1915 when he sent photographs of British submarines in St. John's to the *Toronto Star* and the *Montreal Star*. The items were stopped by Canadian censors and referred to Newfoundland censors. McGrath

---

[39] Ibid.

Parsons Photography Studio on Water Street was one of the two major photo studios in St. John's during WWI censorship in Newfoundland.
(City of St. John's Archives)

complained to the Newfoundland Colonial Secretary's Office questioning why his work was censored while the *Toronto Daily News*, on Saturday, July 10th, published an article taken from a New York newspaper giving more information on the submarines than contained in his article.

McGrath argued that the British submarines were sent to St. John's because the British anticipated the Germans would send their submarines and cruisers to this area. He suggested that news of the presence of submarines in St. John's Harbour would be a deterrent to the Germans.

The journalist noted that because the American newspapers were already quite familiar with the presence of British submarines in St. John's that censorship need not apply to Newfoundland photographers and journalists selling such pictures to the American press. American tourists visited the city weekly on the *Stephano* and the *Florizel* and took photographs and news home with them. The censors did not agree with McGrath and pointed out that the United States was a neutral country and British censors had no control over their press.

Soon after, public notices were issued reminding people of the seriousness of violating the censorship laws. The penalties in Newfoundland were the same as those in England: two years imprisonment and a fine not exceeding $5000. On summary conviction, the penalty was up to six months imprisonment and a fine not exceeding $2000, and the owners of the premises where censor laws were broken were liable to the same. In addition, all printed material and even printing machines could be confiscated.

In Newfoundland, Governor Davis favoured allowing newspaper editors to censor themselves on the conditions that, "... if the law was disregarded a conviction must inevitably follow."[40]

Particular interest was shown by the censors in all letters to the local press from Newfoundland soldiers serving in Gallipoli, following a telegraph from London to the Newfoundland Governor.

The British Colonial Secretary, Bonar Law, issued a special warning in regards to the evacuation of troops at Gallipoli which affected the Newfoundland Regiment. He advised Governor Davidson:

> It is of the greatest importance that the enemy should receive no hint of the strategies by which successful withdrawal of the troops from Anzac and Suvla Coast was effected. No reference whatever should be allowed to appear in the press. Because it is important to assure indiscreet references will not be made in private letters and therefore the only sure way to stop it is to prevent publication of any letter or extract.[41]

The story of the Newfoundland Regiment at Gallipoli is told in Chapter Four.

---

[40] PANL GN2-14.
[41] PANL GN2-14 File #8.

Consequence of Spring Rice Document

By 1918 the secrets confirmed in the Spring Rice Document were a reality. According to the report of the District Commanding Officer (DCO) Home Defence, German submarines were operating in the Atlantic and near Newfoundland shores. The DCO reported to Government that guards were stationed at all cable stations, wireless stations and other vital points. He added that all coastal steamers were armed and fitted with wireless apparatus in order to be able to quickly render reports. The British Admiralty was supervising general patrol and mine-sweeping operations off the coast of Newfoundland.

Mount Pearl Wireless Station under Gunfire

A Memo from the United States Consul to Inspector General of Police, St. John's, September 9, 1918, read:

> On August 27, 1918, an attempt was made by some persons unknown to damage the Marconi Wireless Station at Mount Pearl and to shoot Leading Telegrapher Mooney who turned out to search for the party.[42]

At the start of the war, Imperial Authorities in London viewed the Avalon Peninsula in Newfoundland as a strategic place to set up a wireless telegraph station. The site they chose was Mount Pearl, which after completion was capable of working with Bermuda, Canada, and, at times England, in handling important war communications. The only debate over the station was what to call it. The suggested names were too long. Newfoundland had too many letters and the name Mount Pearl had no significance to strangers. The name Avalon might direct the thoughts of the sender elsewhere and the name St. John's would cause confusion. The one chosen was the 'Marconi Wireless Station,' which had obvious identification potential.

Among the most serious security incidents to occur in Newfoundland during WWI was an incident on August 27, 1918, when two men attacked the Marconi Wireless Station in Mount Pearl, and also attempted to shoot a telegraph operator employed there.

---

[42] PANL GN 2-14 Box 2.

The attackers were detected before they could cause real damage, and a response party from the station gave chase. One of those in that group was Leading Telegrapher Mooney whom the attackers attempted to kill. During the escape pursuit, one of the escapees turned his gun on Mooney attempting to shoot him. Fortunately for Mooney, the bullet missed.

There was an immediate restriction placed on the publication of all information surrounding the attack, and Inspector General of Police Charles Hutchings, acting upon instructions from the Colonial Secretary, initiated an investigation into the attack. Part of his instructions was that if any person or persons considered to be "undesirables" were encountered to deport them.

Around the same time that the Telegraph Station was under attack, Hutchings had received a report from a woman he described as "a prominent person" who had heard a stranger speaking German. The information given by the lady, which was not detailed in the archival report, led police to a Joseph R. Schnitzer. Police felt they were on the right track when Schnitzer met the description of one of the perpetrators given by the guards at the telegraph station. Yet, Police were not anxious to make an arrest. They simply advised him that he was an undesirable and told him to leave the country.

The suspect was not happy with this advice and next day sought and was given a meeting with the Inspector General of Police. Hutchings listened to the man's story but felt it lacked credibility. Schnitzer had told the Inspector General of his business connections and related in detail how he spent his time after working hours.

Hutchings investigated the suspect's story and confirmed his own suspicions. He learned from Schnitzer's nephew that references to his uncle's business connections were untrue. As to Schnitzer's account of his "after work activities", Hutchings concluded, "I considered this ridiculous, and I again invited him to leave the Dominion." Still there was no mention of an arrest and again the suspect expressed reluctance.

To impress Schnitzer with the seriousness of his situation, Hutchings set up another meeting at which time he brought in two guards from the Mount Pearl Telegraph Station to confront him. After meeting the suspect face to face, the two identified him as, "...not only one of the attackers, but he was also the man

THE SPRING RICE DOCUMENT 31

who fired the shot at Mooney." Despite this identification, the man was not arrested, but on the recommendation of Charles Hunt, his lawyer, he was allowed to return to his residence on condition he would report daily to police headquarters. Hunt's request was supported by the American Consul in St. John's, a man named Benedict. The investigation of Schnitzer had extended to Washington and Benedict felt the man should be permitted to stay in Newfoundland until the report from Washington arrived.

While still awaiting the Washington report, Schnitzer made an unscheduled visit to the Inspector General and caught him by complete surprise when he said that despite the American Consul's recommendation that he stay, he was ready to leave the country. Hutchings advised him not to act hastily but to talk the matter over with Benedict. "I don't want any more trouble," Schnitzer replied and said he was leaving Newfoundland on his own accord.[43] Hutchings offered no further explanation as to why with two confirmed eye witness identifications and the statement from the suspect's nephew that the man was not prosecuted. Whether he was acting as a German agent, or else, had a private dispute with someone at the Marconi Wireless Station was not mentioned in archival records reviewed.

As to Schnitzer's nationality, Hutchings reported, "He was born in Jerusalem and probably of German descent as his name indicates. He went to the United States in 1901 and became a naturalized American citizen." Twelve years after, in 1913, he claimed he was a British subject. During the war, Schnitzer's family in Jerusalem were given British protection when "...some notable British official visited there."

Although the incident was kept from the press, rumours of the arrest of German spies and their attempt on the Marconi Wireless Station, although inaccurate, spread and became part of the oral history of WWI.

Bachman
A fisherman from Lunenburg, Nova Scotia who frequented the Grand Banks was alleged to be a German spy because of his German

---

[43] PANL GN 2-14 Box 2. Colonial Secretary's Letters, A letter from the Inspector General of Police, September 9, 1918.

sounding name 'Farbeck or Bachman,' and the fact that he sailed in and out of bays on Newfoundland's southwest coast, an act fishermen interpreted as mapping the area for German submarines.

Because the man was a resident of Nova Scotia, Newfoundland sought Canadian help in investigating him. Results of the Canadian inquiry into the suspect were forwarded to Newfoundland Governor Alex Harris on November 4, 1918, and cleared the man of all suspicion.

The report pointed out that there was no Farbeck at Lunenberg, but several Bachman. The Bachmans were sea captains who frequented the Grand Banks annually from June to September and visited the southwest coast of Newfoundland to gather bait and ice. It stated, "Although their name indicates them to be of German extraction, they have been known Nova Scotian stock for generations back and are all notoriously loyal."[44]

Spy Fever

There is no doubt that the Newfoundland authorities carried out an extensive anti-spy and espionage program throughout Newfoundland and Labrador, and the effort brought in an excessive amount of spy sighting reports which, when investigated, turned out to be futile. Yet, each complaint resulted in a police response.

The following item appeared in the *Evening Telegram* in July 1916 which reflects the widespread net cast by authorities after being alerted by British Intelligence a year earlier of German intentions regarding the Atlantic coast. It read:

> There arrived in the city by train yesterday evening Sergeant Kent in charge of a man named Otto Gower aged thirty-two, who was arrested at Placentia as a prisoner of war, he being alleged to be a full fledged German subject. An investigation was made by the authorities who became satisfied that the suspect was a law student of Halifax, NS and thereupon released him.

Another example of the zealous reporting of these incidents was the case of the alleged spy on Signal Hill which overlooked the Battery and St. John's Harbour.

---

[44] Ibid.

A stranger to the area was observed taking notes describing the harbour and nearby defences. The story spread throughout the Battery and several nearby fishermen brought the matter to the attention of police. The next day when the suspected spy turned up again, he was approached by a police officer.

The complainants watched with interest and they were angered when the police officer took the man's notebook but did not arrest him. Not content with the outcome, a letter was sent to the local newspapers claiming that the police had set free an obvious spy.

It turned out that the man was a Mr. Burke from Military Road, St. John's, who enjoyed sketching pictures of the local scenery and was not a threat to anyone. The exaggerated incident was too much for Jimmy Murphy, local poet, songwriter and often partner of Johnny Burke, the famous Bard of Prescott Street. Murphy responded to those who were "seeing spies everywhere" with the following verses:

The Isle of Fish

When folks are drinking two in one,
today the finest savoured dish
is cod which sticks to every tongue.
Where if a man be looking shy,
some folks will say, he's a German spy.

A man sat on the rocky brow
which overlooks the Battery side.
He watched the boat which sailed below
upon the silent harbour tide.
Not thinking that some had an eye
upon him as a German spy.

They saw him, and they took his work,
two leaves of rhyming it did show.
He gave the German name of Burke
and then they told the spy to go.
Satisfied no bombs would fall from high
and that Burke could be no German spy.

Again we find on Monday night,
Our energetic peelers tramp.
T'was said by some, a German light
but t'was in 'Tom Seymour's' camp.
I am afraid some folks will say— bye n' bye
the man in the moon is a German Spy.

– James Murphy, August 30, 1918
Evening Telegram

Chapter 2

DOUBTED USEFULNESS OF SUBMARINES

While behind the scenes Government was moving to deal with the ominous intelligence warning, a report was received by Governor Davidson that appeared to confirm the contents of the Spring Rice Document. What followed was also an example of the widespread fears over a possible German attack. The now, long forgotten, paramilitary force in Newfoundland known as the Legion of Frontiersmen, whose history is recorded in chapter three, met with an unexpected reception from a local population when they responded to the report.

On August 1st, Governor Davidson received a message from Conche noting that a submarine periscope had been sighted near Groais Island. Residents there tried to alert a passing steamer of their sighting but failed to get its attention. Groais Island and the intelligence that enemy submarines would be in the area in late July and early August were mentioned in the Spring Rice Document, a fact of primary interest to the Governor.

Governor Davidson was concerned over the possibility of panic among the residents. He had already dispatched the SS *Fogota* which was manned by police and members of the Newfoundland Regiment. The vessel was armed with a twelve-pounder field gun and a three-pounder from HMS *Calypso*. However, before they arrived on the scene a near tragic situation involving the Legion of Frontiersmen developed.

The Legion of Frontiersmen, who wore unusual uniforms including an Australian type hat, had become aware of the sighting and, rapidly responded, arriving on the scene before the *Fogota*. Coastal residents had been advised to keep a sharp lookout from La Scie to Flower's Cove and orders were given to arrest and detain all suspicious-looking strangers.

Unfortunately, not all communities were aware of the existence of the Frontiersmen or their rather unusual uniform. Neither had they seen a German in uniform. When the Frontiersmen were sighted approaching one particular place, the villagers thought the enemy had landed and they prepared to do battle. Armed to the teeth with old rifles and shotguns, these patriots were ready to repel the invaders from Newfoundland soil.

The residents had mistaken the Frontiersmen for Germans. The commanding officer of the Frontiersmen quickly convinced the resistance force that they were not German soldiers. This was followed with apologies and the extension of true Newfoundland hospitality to the Frontiersmen.

The Submarine was a New War Weapon

At the outbreak of WWI, submarines were not held in high regard as military weapons by the British. In July 1914, the following memo was written by the Royal Navy Assistant Director of Naval Operations:

> The submarine has the smallest value of any vessel for the direct attack upon trade. She does not carry a crew which is capable of taking charge of a prize, she cannot remove passengers and other persons if she wishes to sink one.[1] At first, the Germans promoted the submarine, not as a weapon of war, but as a "submersible freighter," a new idea that was going to use large submarines as cargo transport vessels. Almost a year before the breakout of war with Britain, the

The first German U-Boat of the model known as Deutschland was the first to be captured in WWI. Germans argued these were designed to carry civilian cargo and were not weapons of war. Another of the same model was in Baltimore in July 1916. (IWM)

---

[1] John Abbatiello, <u>Anti-Submarine Warfare in WWI</u>.

Germans were experimenting with the use of these non-armed submarines. One of these was the *Deutschland* which was captured after it experienced engine trouble off the Irish coast. Others were being used to cross the Atlantic and in June 1916, the arrival of a German merchant submarine in Baltimore Harbour, Maryland, attracted a great deal of public attention. The crew of that submarine was terrified over the return trip to Germany because they were convinced the British had laid anti-submarine netting outside the three mile limit.

Captain Koenig, master of the super submarine, announced before leaving Baltimore that the "submersible freighter" is the first of a fleet of such craft built to ply regularly in the trans-Atlantic trade. He told the press, "This is not the only one that is coming. Just wait, there will be more here soon, and we are going back for another cargo. We are going to have a regular line."[2]

As military weapons, submarines were generally viewed as being unproven, too slow, too easily caught on the surface, too limited in range and likely a waste of money. Author Harris Brayton in his book *The Navy Times: Book of Submarines* pointed out:

Perhaps a submarine could serve as a picket, locate the enemy, and send a message via wireless radio (if not more than forty miles from a receiving station) or carrier pigeon, with coordinates, course and speed. Under international law, she could not do much else.

Law and U-boats

At the outbreak of war, international scholars around the world were still wrestling with the question as to whether or not "...a submarine is a ship of war or not." Some felt that all the legalities related to the new vessel might not be settled until after the war. An item in the *Evening Telegram* on July 11, 1916, observed:

It will not be of much more than academic interest. We know what British opinion will be if they can lay hands on the Deutschland (1ˢᵗ freighter submarine). The matter of

---

[2] The Evening Telegram, July 1916.

armament seems to be assuming altogether too much importance; It should only be relevant where a ship of a recognised peaceful type such as a merchantman is claimed by the enemy to be a ship of war. The submarine is like the cruiser, a ship of war, and it should not matter whether she is armed or not.

Outlaw Submarines

In the years leading up to WWI, there was an international effort to outlaw the use of submarine warfare. Although the issue was considered at the 1st Haig Peace Conference in 1899, it was not until 1908 at the 2nd Haig Peace Conference that a decision was finally made. The conference issued what became known as the "London Declaration" which deemed that the submarine be governed by the same "Prize Rules" that traditionally applied to cruisers and other ships of war. It gave submarines power to stop and search ships suspected of carrying illegal war materials. If contraband was found on a ship, the submarine had the right to sink it but only after assuring the following conditions were applied:

> First, it had to be an enemy ship; secondly, the passengers and crew were to be provided with the supplies and necessities needed to enable them to reach safety. These items included: lifeboats, navigational equipment and other items necessary for a safe voyage. A neutral ship could be seized but had to be escorted to port and held.[3]

Submarine History

The German military had knowledge of the possibility of submarines as early as 1850 when Wilhelm Bauer invented the first practical submarine called the *Brandtaucher*. Naval strategists concluded that the development offered little in the way of military value, and the submarine was not considered again by the Germans until 1906. During the interim years, Germany engaged in a "naval arms race" with the British. By then, other major powers were already building military submarines and the German Navy was the last power to join the race. Its first submarine was the U-1 which was launched in 1906. Experimentation with the military possibilities

---

[3] Brayton Harris, <u>The Navy Times Book of Submarines</u>, p160, 161.

of a submarine led, in 1912, to the start of production of a fleet of U-boats.

By the time war broke out in August 1914, the Imperial German Navy had twenty U-boats in service and were expecting fifteen more to be delivered. The major efforts of the U-boats in WWI were carried out in the North Sea and the North Atlantic.[4]

In 1914, the total number of submarines in the world was 282.[5] Because Germany was late in catching up to other major countries in this area, she gained an advantage through the lessons learned by other navies. At the time war broke out, according to author Brayton Harris, "Ship for ship she was notably superior, with better armor, higher speed and a larger throw weight of armament."

Among the major powers, Germany had the smallest submarine fleet but it proved to be the strongest in war as the fleet increased its numbers.

Churchill Outwitted Germans

In anticipation of the British declaring war, the Germans tied up their entire U-boat fleet but were outwitted by the British Navy under the Lord of the Admiralty, Winston Churchill. They had calculated that Britain's naval policy would be to attack immediately after war was declared. They were certain Churchill would send the Grand Fleet to attack the U-boat fleet which the British outnumbered almost three to one.

Churchill had decided on a different strategy and even surprised the British War Cabinet by giving it a go ahead at 11:00 p.m. August 4th British time. His strategy was to order the entire Grand Fleet to sea to avoid possible surprise attacks upon it by the enemy. This was one hour before the midnight deadline Britain gave Germany to get out of Belgium or face war with England.

Meanwhile, the German U-boat fleet waited and waited but were perplexed that the British did not come! German naval strategists in Berlin concluded:

---

[4] David Miller, U-boats: History, Development and Equipment 1914-1945.
[5] On the eve of WWI, the following list shows the size of each of the major power's submarine fleet:
A. United Kingdom: Seventy-four in service, fifty-five under construction or pending construction.
B. France: Sixty-two in service and nine under construction.
C. Russia- Forty-eight in service. All purchased from United States, England, France and   D. United States: Thirty in service, ten under construction.
E. Germany: Twenty-eight in service, four under construction

The British Main Fleet and probably all war vessels which
are worth attacking by U-boats are so far away from
Germany that it is beyond the technical capacities of our
U-boats to find them. Neither is it possible for U-boats to
lie in wait off the bases for long periods owing to their
distance from Germany. U-boat operations will therefore
be abandoned for the present.[6]

A month passed before the U-boat fleet came in contact with
the Grand Fleet. The British who were ready to take on the U-boat
fleet in direct battle changed their policy after the surprising
success of one U-boat on September 22, 1914. On that date, one
of the fleet's older boats, the *U-9*, sank three British cruisers. This
was a significant victory because more British soldiers died in the
battle against the *U-9* than were lost by Lord Nelson in all his
battles put together. The Grand Fleet's Commander-in-Chief,
Admiral Jellicoe, advised Churchill:

> It is suicidal to forego our advantageous position in the big
> ships by risking them in waters infested with submarines.
> The result might quite easily be such weakening of our
> battle fleet and battle cruiser strength as seriously to
> jeopardize the future of the country by giving over to the
> Germans the command of the open seas.[7]

Germans Face Serious Challenges
The war was not going well for Germany by the fall of 1916.
Britain's blockade of supplies was hampering their war effort and
causing serious problems at home. Germany's high expectations of
being able to defeat Britain's Grand Fleet had greatly diminished.
The German army was experiencing enormous casualties in the
Battles of Verdum and the Somme. Setting up a counter blockade
against England using the German U-boat fleet was believed by
strategists to be the best way to change the course of the war.
Germany was worried that the accidental or unintended
sinking of an American ship would bring the United States into
the war on Britain's side. There was a similar concern over the

---

[6] Brayton Harris, <u>The Navy Times Book of Submarines</u>.
[7] Ibid.

same thing happening to Denmark or the Netherlands which would open up a new front.

Up to January 1917, German U-boats engaged in surface attacks using its deck guns, however, this strategy changed to the use of underwater torpedo attacks which presented a greater problem for the allies. The change brought immediate and impressive results. In just three months, the U-boats sank 977 British ships.

Its success was short-lived, and the strategy backfired when on April 6, 1917, the United States declared war on Germany. The Allies were further strengthened by adopting the recommendation of Winston Churchill that they use convoys as a means of dealing with the U-boat threat.

In respect to the use of convoys, author- historian David Miller suggests that the German U-boat command failed to seize upon an opportunity that might have affected the outcome of WWI:

> The use of convoys was, without doubt, the key to the allies success, but the escorts were equipped with only the most basic sensors-hydro- phones-which gave them little chance of locating U-boats. Radios were not as sophisticated in 1917 as in 1939-1942, but they were installed in many U-boats and there seems to be no reason why 'Wolf-Pack' tactics could not have worked, indeed, they might have overwhelmed the escorts and wrought havoc among the convoys. That opportunity was to be taken twenty-two years later, however.[8]

The problem allies experienced in battling the aggressive U-boat fleet was the difficulty in finding them. The hydrophone in use at the time could detect the noise from a submarine's propellor but had limited success because it could not eliminate other underwater sounds.

Indicator nets seemed to be a sound anti-submarine weapon but failed in practice. These nets measured 300 ft (100m) long and thirty-three ft. (10m) deep, and were made of steel wire. They were towed across U-boat routes and if a U-boat became entangled in one, a flare was used to attract a patrol vessel to the site to sink it.

---

[8] David Miller, U-Boat History-Development and Equipment, 1914-1945.

The Americans developed what was known as the "Pattern" camouflage to confuse the U-boat's visual firing controls. In time, other navies adopted the American "haze grey" camouflage for their surface ships. (National Archives)

The British Navy, at that stage in the war, concluded that the only effective way of overcoming the U-boat threat was either to ram it, or to use gunfire. One tactic the British adopted was to camouflage and arm merchant ships. When a U-boat approached one with expectations to capture or sink it, the gun coverings were removed and the surprised U-boat was attacked. The camouflaged boats were called Q-boats. These succeeded in sinking eleven U-boats but, in doing so, lost twenty -seven Q-boats.

In 1915, the British introduced depth charges. These sank twenty-six U-boats. In addition to the depth charges, they discovered that anti-submarine minefields were effective in anti-submarine warfare and in protecting the coastlines of Britain and its allies.

No More U-boat Doubts by UK

Any doubts the British had about the U-boat threat changed in the first months of the war when German U-boats scored several quick successes against the Royal Navy. On September 5th, *U-21* torpedoed the British cruiser *Pathfinder*. Three British cruisers were sunk on September 22nd by *U-9*. These were the *Aboukir*, the *Cressy* and the *Hogue*.

The Captain of *U-17* was chivalrous in his treatment of the crew and passengers of the SS *Glitra* when, on October 20, 1914, he seized and sank it. He scrupulously followed the "Prize Rules" by insisting on verifying the ship's papers and then he took action to evacuate all on board in lifeboats before removing the seacocks which caused the ship to sink. He then towed the lifeboats to a point just a few miles off the coast of Norway. Less than a week later, the *U-24* sank the French ship *Admiral Ganteume*, after mistaking it for a troop ship.[9]

Britain's strategy during this stage of the war was its traditional plan of action against an enemy on the continent by blocking its ports to prevent supplies from getting through or exports from leaving. This worked well up to 1915. In February 1915, Germany implemented its plan to attack British shipping and they declared all waters around Britain as a War Zone. However, ships from Neutral countries were exempted. This strategy was unsuccessful because of the superiority of the British Navy.

This U-boat era was brought to a close by three incidents. The *Lusitania* with 1201 passengers including 128 Americans was torpedoed by the *U-20* and sparked worldwide outrage, but not enough to bring the US into the war. To calm the neutral Americans, Germany promised that there would be no more attacks on passenger ships. However, despite the assurances, two more liners were sunk: the *Arabic* on August 19th and the *Hesperia* on September 6th. The total number lost in both sinkings was seventy-six of which three were Americans. While one era of U-boat activity came to an end, it was not the last of the U-boat threat.

Germans Sank Newfoundland Passenger Vessel-1916

On October 9, 1916, just two miles off the Nantucket coast of the United States, the German *U-53* submarine sank the *Stephano*, a Newfoundland passenger ship. She was the sister-ship of the *Florizel*. It was not a surprise sinking because the U-boat fired four shots across the *Stephano's* bow to bring her to a stop. The U-boat Captain then ordered the vessel's Captain to instruct his sixty-seven crew members and ninety-seven passengers, which included some Americans, to abandon ship. The Germans went on board and looted the ship of all its valuables.

The unique thing about this drama at sea was that the entire episode was carried out in the presence of twenty-eight American

---

[9]John Abbatiello, <u>Anti-Submarine Warfare in World War I</u>.

Naval vessels. One of the US Destroyers accommodated a German request to move aside to enable the *U-53* to get a clean shot at the Newfoundland vessel. The Americans obliged. Yet, there was little they could do, because the United States was still a neutral country, and a confrontation with the German U-boat could have sparked a war.

The US *Balch*, a destroyer, took all the passengers and crew from the *Stephano* before it was fired upon. The firing of twenty-seven shots into the ship's hull had little effect. The U-boat then fired a torpedo which broke the ship in two causing her to sink quickly. American Lt. Carey later told the press that, at first, the German guns did not do any real damage, "...but, they gave us some beautiful fireworks to gaze at. After they fired the torpedo, there was nothing else to do. We waved good-bye to the Germans and shaped our course for Newport."

When the story hit the American press some critics claimed that the German action was illegal. Some American lawyers argued that the sub should have been interned in an American port before she could do any damage. George Wallace of Freeport, New York, asked, "What kind of officers were in charge of these war vessels. Even if the passengers had not been Americans, any of our old-time seaworthies would have rushed to the rescue in the cause of common humanity."[10]

Between October 7-9, 1915, the same German *U-53* sank nine British merchant ships off Rhode Island in international waters.

Armed Fishing Vessels on Grand Banks

Protecting the fishing fleets on the Grand Banks was a major problem in 1917 and 1918 due to the increased capabilities of the German U-boats, which earlier in the war were restricted to the European coasts. In February 1918, an allied conference was held regarding the need for mutual cooperation in protecting the fishing fleets on the Newfoundland Grand Banks in view of the hostile submarine activities off the North American coast. Protection of the Labrador fishery, which operated between mid-June and early October, was needed only at the fleet's assembly point at Battle Harbour.

---

[10] Jack Fitzgerald, <u>Strange but True Newfoundland Stories</u>, Creative Publishers.

The country most prepared to deal with this German threat was France. Their plan involved an eighty-two vessel fishing fleet with each vessel armed with guns and munitions, and smoke producing appliances. The fleet would sail to the Grand Banks in convoys and be accompanied through danger zones by armed trawlers and then move onto the Grand Banks. After arriving at their destination, they would be met by eight auxiliary motored schooners armed with guns, two bomb mortars and searchlights. Canada and the United States adopted the French plan but on a smaller scale.[11]

It was jointly agreed that at the banks the Nova Scotian and American vessels would keep in one group and the armed vessels allotted distributed as follows: four to the coast off Nova Scotia, four to the coast off the United States and four to remain at the Grand Banks. In addition, one patrol vessel for each country was provided.

The military did not feel that the fisheries were liable to an ongoing attack, but considering the extension of the danger zone and the increase in size and radius of submarine action, a real menace existed especially where steamer routes crossed the fishing grounds.[12]

Victim of U-boat attack tells his story

Although there was a U-boat presence and threat off the North American coast since 1915, the real threat came in 1918 when the Germans pursued more aggressive submarine warfare in that area. August 1918 proved to be a particular busy month for sightings and encounters with enemy submarines. The SS *Erik* which was 583 tons, with a St. John's crew, was torpedoed off St. Pierre while on a trip to pick up a cargo of coal at Nova Scotia. The submarine rescued the crew and transferred them to the *Willie G* which carried them to safety. The *Erik* was owned by James Baird & Co. of St. John's.

When the *Erik* was attacked by a German U-boat, the telegraph operator on the schooner was Chesley Ryan, a three-year veteran of the Royal Newfoundland Regiment who had fought in Gallipoli and in the Battle of the Somme in France. Several days after the schooner was sunk by a U-boat, Ryan was in St. John's where he

---

[11] Ibid.
[12] Ibid.

gave a detailed account of how the attack unfolded and the German's treatment of the crew of Newfoundlanders.

His absorbing account of this encounter with the enemy so near his own homeland was reported in the *Evening Telegram* on September 2, 1918. It read:

It was 1:00 a.m. on Sunday, August 25th, when I was in the land of dreams. A loud explosion, seemingly from the engine room, caused me to spring out of my bunk in the wireless cabin and run down to the deck. A Russian Finlander, who was at the wheel, ran up shouting, 'Stop the engines! Stop the engines! Submarine!' A shell then screamed across our stern and burst in the water a hundred yards away.

I went around to see where all the men were when the cabin windows came in with a click and the lamp was blown out. A shell had burst on the derrick and wounded the mate, who was on the bridge. The same shell cut the derrick and it dropped to the deck. It also carried away a lot of the rigging and part of the wireless aerial.

I left the cabin and went forward to the forecastle and then several shells hit the ship in quick succession around the engine room. The boiler was letting off steam, and shots of flame made their appearance around the smoke stack. We thought that the ship was on fire, but the flames died down when the firing ceased.

The deck was honeycombed by shellfire, and it was dangerous to move around. Nobody saw the sub until she hove up alongside over half an hour later. She was firing from the port side as the flashes from her gun revealed and all the shots were falling aft. Our two lifeboats were smashed and a little punt with one side half blown away looked to us as our only means of salvation. Some of the men rowed off to the submarine that was now plainly in view on our port side.

She looked about three hundred feet in length and carried two 5.9 guns; a wireless aerial was plainly visible aft of the coning tower. Her deck was crowded with Huns (Germans) all eager to get a glance at their victims. Our boat was now rowing back to the *Erik*, and we dropped a ladder over the side to let the Hun officer on board. He had two sailors with him who carried a large bomb to complete the ship's destruction.

The Captain handed over his papers to the Hun whilst the firemen and sailors were working hard to plug the big lifeboat with blankets and nail on some boards. But the boat was useless and would not keep us afloat. I went back to the wireless cabin and found the two Hun sailors with a flashlight taking all the electrical fittings and stowing them in my valise. Part of the apparatus was lying on the floor having dropped from the wall because of the concussion of the shells. The windows were all smashed. I managed to find my uniform, cap and coat.

The submarine again came up in speaking distance and the Huns speaking in their own gibberish, told the boarding officer to send us on to the submarine. The little punt was half full of water and needed continuous bailing to keep afloat. I made two trips in her with the men and the last trip we brought of the Germans who had set the time fuse of the bomb.

I was the second last member of our crew to get on the submarine and as I was about to get down the manhole, the bomb on the *Erik* burst. I didn't see her sink. Down behind the submerging apparatus of the submarine, we were all stowed. It was now about 4:30 p.m. The Hun engineers gave some of the men coffee, but no water was to be had.

It was now raining and a little fishing vessel the *Willie G* from Grand Bank was anchored close by. We were taken off in dories and placed on board the schooner. If she had a few more dories, the Huns would have sent her to the bottom and let us row to land, but as luck would have it the *Willie G* with her six dories was allowed to go.

I went in the forecastle and had some breakfast, and when I came on deck again the submarine was quite a few miles away. The rain was still pouring and cleared up about 10:00 p.m. We could now see St. Pierre to the southeast and some bankers on our starboard. At noon, I noticed that only one banker could be seen and they were all anchored at ten o'clock. A few minutes later the problem was solved because Mr. Submarine was up alongside the remaining banker, the *J.J. O'Flaherty* from Gloucester. We watched her sink stern first. We met some of their dory men before and warned them of the submarine, but the warnings came too late.

The *Willie G* moved off, and headed for the safety of St. Pierre just twenty-five to thirty miles away.

U-boat Captain a good host

On August 31, 1918, a U-boat sank the schooner *Elsie Porter*. The captain, his son and a crewman of the schooner were taken aboard the submarine and treated kindly by the German officers and crew who gave them coffee. The Newfoundland captain later said that they were given the very best and kindest treatment by the German captain.

The German commander questioned the three about the state of the fishery, their business and families. The captain was invited into the officers' quarters and given refreshments, food, cigars and cigarettes. He later told reporters, "The bread eaten by the officers was good white bread, while that of the crew was black and preserved in tins– not very fresh and tasted stale."

The Newfoundland captain noted that when chatting with the German crew, they were told that the men were fed up with the war and wished it was over. They expressed a desire to be able to go ashore. After almost four hours on the submarine, the Commander released them. Their dory with food, water and clothing had been tied to the U-boat.

All three oars in the dory broke, and the men had to rely on its sail at times when it was appropriate to use. They rowed and sailed 180 miles and were finally rescued when the schooner *Harry Lewis* picked them up two miles outside St. John's. They were given a mug-up on board the schooner before going ashore in St. John's.

The rescued captain told reporters that before leaving the submarine the Hun captain wished them "God speed and good luck." In St. John's they stayed at the Seaman's Institute. The schooner was valued at $5000.[13]

Other Submarine Encounters

According to the *Evening Telegram* on June 9, 1918, the Boston schooner *Jacob M. Haskell* was torpedoed off the Atlantic coast. The item noted that the Germans were under orders to sink every American ship they could find, but to spare all lives possible. The Americans were picked up at sea by the SS *Grecian* and brought to Boston.

Gustav Nelsen, an American passenger, told reporters, "The sub's commander spoke perfect English, and was so very polite that he got on our nerves." The German Captain followed international law by first asking for the ship's papers. He then ordered that the American flag be taken down. He told the passengers and crew, "We don't want your ships. You have three minutes to get away from her before we sink your ship."

Miss M. McCurdy who had served as a stewardess on the *Florizel* lost her life when a German submarine torpedoed the *Carolina* off the Virginia Capes on the Atlantic coast during June 1918. The attack on a passenger ship drew strong criticism in New York where the treatment of passengers and crews was compared to the unusual polite behaviour accorded to those Americans who came ashore from the first half dozen ships torpedoed in that area.

In the case of the *Carolina*, the Germans forced its people, women and children included, into open boats and left them 150 miles from land. The *New York Times* observed, "In civilized warfare when the captured cannot be taken aboard the submarine either the ship is not sunk or the wireless is used to summon help for the victims. German chivalry–that returns a strong man's umbrella and leaves a woman to die in an open boat!"

The *Bianca*, owned by Bowring Brothers, was torpedoed on August 26, 1918, in Sambro Head, Nova Scotia. The U-boat crew

---

[13] The Evening Telegram, September 18, 1918, p5.

Censor laws prohibited the publishing of photos of British submarines in St. John's Harbour during WWI. Violation of the law carried a heavy fine or a jail term, or both. This photo shows a British submarine leaving St. John's Harbour followed by the troop ship *Calgarian*. (PANL)

took all the crew's extra clothing before allowing them to abandon ship. The ship's captain was Mark Burke, and all the crew were from Carbonear. Burke was more than surprised when he learned a week later that the *Bianca* had not sunk, but was claimed as 'prize' by the Boston trawler *Commonwealth*. The shock of the torpedo hit had damaged her but the hull withstood the impact. The vessel was carrying 130,000 pounds of cod and a cargo of tobacco. The *Commonwealth* captain claimed $125,000 prize money. The *Bianca* was repaired at the St. John's dry dock and reclaimed by Captain Burke for its owners.

Also, in August, three vessels from Lunenburg, Nova Scotia, were torpedoed near the St. Pierre Banks after the crews were allowed to abandon ship in lifeboats. These vessels were: *C.B.Walters, Ferma B. Adams,* and the *E.W. Walters*.[14]

On August 27, 1918, the vessel *Terra Nova* arrived at Bell Island from Sydney, Nova Scotia with some alarming news for authorities at Bell Island. R. D. Walsh told Superintendent D. Stott that a German submarine had sunk five Lunenburg schooners shortly

---

[14] The Evening Telegram August 29, 30, 1918.

before the *Terra Nova* arrived there. During the same month, a U-boat torpedoed the Norwegian steamer *Bergsdalen* 120 miles off Cape Race. The steamer sank within three minutes after being hit. The crew had time enough to launch two lifeboats; those who didn't make it to the lifeboats jumped over the side. They were rescued by the others and made it to Cape Race. From there, they went by way of Cape Broyle to St. John's. No loss of life was recorded in the incident.

In the same week, a Newfoundland seaman on the Whaler *Port Saunders* reported seeing a U-boat seventeen miles southwest of Cape Broyle Head.[15] In August, the Colonial Secretary's office in St. John's was informed that the Germans had laid mines on the Atlantic coast. On August 30, 1918, Ken and Joe Parsons, fishermen, were setting their trawls on the south west end of Bell Island when they saw a submarine periscope nearby. They reported this to authorities but the sub was not identified.

On September 12, 1918, Richard Murphy of the Newfoundland Post Telegraph Company reported to the Colonial Secretary that a submarine was seen in the bay by two men near Stephenville about one mile off Bankhead. He said, "It was 300 feet long with a square thing in the middle."[16] The Magistrate at St. George's took sworn statements from the two witnesses, a Mr. Cook and a Mr. King.

What could have been disastrous for shipping near St. John's harbour was averted because of a major mistake made by a U-boat captain. According to Bob Carew of St. John's, who researched the operation of the Marconi Telegraph Station at Mount Pearl, on August 11, 1918 German submarine *U-155* was sent out from Kiel, Germany, to, among other targets, lay mines off St. John's, Newfoundland and Halifax, Nova Scotia. Fortunately, Captain Ferdinand Studt of the *U-155* misread the orders and made an unsuccessful attempt to lay the mines of St. John, New Brunswick.

Government Warnings About Submarines
All merchant ships were warned that if confronted by a submarine to head for the nearest port. They were advised to keep the submarine in view and watch for bubbles which would show

---

[15] The Evening Telegram August 30, 1918, p7.
[16] PANL Colonial Secretary's Letters. GN 2/14 Box 2.

the pathway of any torpedo that was fired. Zigzagging, the warning said, "could avoid a hit."[17]

The authorities did take action in anticipation that submarines or raiders might attack St. John's. The Prime Minister approved the following press release:

> 1. In the (unlikely) event of an attack on St. John's by an enemy raider, an alarm will be sounded at once. 2. The signal in case of alarm will consist of fifteen strokes, repeated at least three times on the fire alarm bell at the Central Fire Station and the West End Fire Station and on St. Thomas' Church bells and St. Joseph's Church bells for the east end. 3. When the alarm is sounded– stay where you are and keep indoors. Do not go to cellars.[18]

The Government of Canada, aware of the sightings of German submarines in Newfoundland waters, asked the Newfoundland Government to help them by posting notices in telegraph offices throughout the colony requesting fishermen and others to keep a special lookout for submarines and to report sightings immediately to the nearest telegraph office. Allied suggestions that Newfoundland consider maintaining a permanent fleet of mine sweepers was a program beyond the Colony's financial resources. The Governor explained that all ships leaving St. John's were given information regarding the positions of known submarines and of mines laid. Courses for them to steer were recommended.

End Result

The intended great U-boat offensive on the North American coast that started in May 1918 turned out to be futile and of little military value. The successes included the torpedoing of fishing schooners, coal scows, a few coastal vessels and one obsolete warship. When widespread reports of sightings of U-boats, followed by news of their attacks, reached the public there was general concern. As the nature of the attacks was made known, the public went from considering the U-boat a menace to viewing it as a nuisance.

---

[17] PANL G1-10/0 Reel 2.
[18] Ibid.

An editorial comment in the *Evening Telegram* on August 2, 1918, observed:

> The spectacle of a submarine in combat with a tug and barges off Cape Cod threw the whole affair into comic relief. Especially, considering the great military lanes through which travelled one and a quarter million troops and incredible amounts of ammunition and supplies have passed.

Chapter 3

FROM A DISMAL START

Feared German Naval Attack on St. John's Harbour

The declaration of war on August 4, 1914, at 9:25 p.m. Newfoundland time, was not a complete surprise to Sir Walter Davidson, Governor of Newfoundland. Just a week before, on July 29th, the British Government had notified Davidson to "Adopt Precautionary Stage." A follow up message ordered him to call out the Royal Navy Reserve (RNR) and lay the groundwork for censorship throughout the colony. However, what happened on the first day of the war caught him off guard and heightened anxiety among elected Government representatives.

The reason for the sudden pressure was the information received from the British Admiralty that the German cruiser *Dresden* was within striking distance of St. John's Harbour and an attack seemed imminent.

The crisis deteriorated when, following the British Admiralty's suggestion, Davidson attempted to mobilize the Colony's only military force, the Royal Naval Reserve. The RNR were well trained and were fine marksmen. They had undergone instruction and battle drills on the training vessel, the H.M.S. *Briton* stationed in St. John's Harbour. However, when the Governor attempted to mobilize the force, only seventy Reservists responded. It was summertime, and the others were at the fishing grounds. A reading of Davidson's logbook for August 4, 1914, reveals just how seriously the matter was considered at that time. He noted:

> We are all determined that if the German cruiser *Dresden* enters the harbour of St. John's, we shall block the entrance to the narrows by sinking two of our own ships in the fairway; and if the *Dresden* threatens retaliation, to announce that in the event of its opening fire on the town and arresting or executing the Governor and leading people as prisoners or hostages, the people are armed and will exact the fullest retribution on the whole crew; but that if the cruiser surrenders before the advent of a superior force, the capitulation will be accepted on the following terms, namely, that the safety and personal

effects of the officers and men will be guaranteed and that they will be transported to a neutral territory, but that the ship is not be sunk or blown up.[1]

According to the Admiralty's warning, the *Dresden* was in waters off St. Pierre just 250 miles from St. John's. In anticipation of an attack on St. John's, the British Navy sent a cruiser from Bermuda. While Newfoundland officials watched the developing situation with much concern, word came that dispelled the anxiety as quickly as it had started. Further investigations by the British Admiralty had determined that the report regarding the *Dresden* being in Newfoundland waters was erroneous. The German cruiser was actually heading for South American waters to attack shipping there. Yet, the legitimate concern over a German threat to the Atlantic seaboard remained, and the cruiser from Bermuda continued on to patrol the Newfoundland and Canadian coastline.

Historian G. W. Nicholson said the incident, "...was a bold decision and one that illustrates the resourcefulness and iron resolution of the man who for the next three years was to play a leading role in the prosecution of Newfoundland's war effort."

Newfoundland at War 1914

The spark that set off WWI was ignited on June 28, 1914, when a Serbian nationalist assassinated the Archduke Francis Ferdinand, heir to the Austro-Hungarian throne. It was on that date that German troops entered Belgium, totally disregarding the ultimatum from Britain that Germany respect Belgian territory and neutrality. At midnight, Britain declared war on Germany, which also meant that Newfoundland, as a colony, was at war. On August 31, 1914, the Germans entered France and took Amiens on the Somme River creating the scene for some of the war's greatest battles and the Newfoundland Regiment's place in military history.[2]

While things were deteriorating in Europe leading up to the outbreak of war, Germany was carefully assessing British military strength and the loyalty and commitment of the dominions and colonies of the Empire. They were confident that if England went

---

[1] G.W. Nicholson, <u>The Fighting Newfoundlander</u>.
[2] H. Robert Ferrell, general editor, <u>Twentieth Century, An Almanac</u>.

to war, it could not depend on others in the British Empire to provide any significant military strength to its efforts. The loyalty of India and Ireland to Britain was in doubt, and there were problems in other parts of the Empire with developing independence movements, their remoteness, and lack of military organizations and preparedness for a war.[3]

The Royal Navy Reserve

Following the withdrawal of British troops in 1871, Newfoundland made no effort to build a military force of its own. When the Boer War broke out in 1899, Newfoundland was the only country in the Empire that did not have a military. While all the others were sending forces to stand by the British in Africa, Newfoundland was conspicuous by its absence.

Embarrassed by the situation, Newfoundland Governor Sir Henry McCallum expressed his regret. He informed the Colonial Office that the failure was not due to lack of loyalty on the part of Newfoundlanders, but that "Newfoundland simply had no trained forces available."[4]

There was little public support for the Boer War among Newfoundlanders and when the Governor tried to form a battalion of rifle volunteers, lack of interest forced him to abandon the idea.

In 1902, with the Boer War over, Governor Sir Cavendish Boyle proceeded to improve Newfoundland's military situation by organizing its own Royal Naval Reserve of 600 men. In turn, Prime Minister Sir Robert Bond advised the British Admiralty that Newfoundland's action was evidence of its intentions to contribute to the cost of defence within its means. England supplied a training vessel for the new reserve unit.

Over the past 100 years, the names *Calypso* and *Briton* have been used in describing the training vessel of the Royal Naval Reserve in Newfoundland. Originally, the training vessel was named the H.M.S. *Calypso* and it arrived in St. John's from England on October 15, 1902. Soon after the outbreak of the war, it was renamed the H.M.S. *Briton.* This has led to the longtime confusion over the vessel's correct name.

---

[3] PANL MG 439 Box 1.
[4] PANL GN-2/38, GN2/5.

This vessel was launched in 1883 as a third-class cruiser of 2770 tons. It had 4020 horsepower, could travel 14.6 knots and carried a crew of 293 men when in commission. In 1922, it was sold to A. H. Murray & Co., who converted it into a coal storage boat.[5]

When war broke out in 1914, Newfoundland's only military force was the Royal Naval Reserve. Yet, this colony was the first in the Empire to respond to the Mother Country's call to arms and in just sixty days had raised a full regiment of volunteers to go overseas.

Two days after war broke out, Governor Davidson, following consultation with his ministers, sent a message to London to notify them that Newfoundland was about to recruit men to serve in the military. Its plan involved: (1) the recruitment of a force of 1000 men for the Royal Naval Reserve by October 31st to serve abroad for one year with Newfoundland paying all local expenses; (2) Several hundred efficient local brigade members had offered to enlist for land service abroad, (3) A commitment to raise an additional 500 men to form a Regiment in one month, and (4) To recruit men between eighteen and thirty-six years to train for home defence. These men would later be used for additional drafts for the Newfoundland Regiment.

Davidson received a reply from London which caused serious confusion within the Royal Naval Reserve in St. John's. The British gladly accepted Newfoundland's offer to raise a Regiment, but needed more time to reply on the offer regarding the Naval Reserve.

Discouraged by the hesitation regarding the Naval Reserve, the 1000 men who offered to serve were discharged and sent home. Reservists who were already serving on the *Calypso* were also sent home. The Newfoundland Patriotic Association was surprised by the hesitation, and Association member, William Higgins, pointed out that the need to supply men for the navy was a defence priority. The matter was cleared up almost two weeks later when the Admiralty advised the Governor of its gratitude and it accepted the proposal to increase the RNR to 1000.[6]

In addition to the pay promised the volunteers, which was $1.05 per day, the Admiralty promised that members would share

---

[5] H.M. Mosdell, M.B., <u>What Year Was That?</u>
[6] PANL MG 632, <u>Minutes of Patriotic Association of Newfoundland</u>.

in prize money after the war. This was a reference to the proceeds from the sale of ships captured and sold during and after the war. The *Calypso* was used as a headquarters for the Royal Navy Reserve. It was restricted from going to sea under her own steam because its boilers needed to be replaced. The vessel, which was 220 feet long, was tied up at the King's Wharf and used as a barracks for the Royal Navy Reserve.[7]

Boy Cadet Corps a Military Asset

The Royal Navy Reserve was not the only source of military strength when war broke out in 1914. There was a reserve of another kind whose value was not readily apparent, but which became obvious within the first year of the war. The several cadet corps in the colony had a surprising contribution to make. Without it, Newfoundland could not have responded as rapidly as it did in raising a full Regiment and sending it to Britain within sixty days after war erupted.

These boys' brigades had already built a reservoir of young men with physical, disciplinary and even marksmanship training. Archival records show that all the original officers of the Newfoundland Regiment and practically all the non-commissioned officers were officers and noncommissioned officers of these brigades.

The brigades, apart from the Legion of Frontiersmen which made a contribution of its own, were: the Church Lads Brigade (CLB), The Catholic Cadet Corps (CCC), The Methodist Guards (MG), and the Newfoundland Highlanders (NH). The Church Lads Brigade after the war became affiliated with the King's Royal Rifles and was officially recognized as a cadet unit. The Catholic Cadet Corps, Highlanders and Methodist Guards operated under individual local arrangements.

In Britain, such boys' brigades were affiliated with the different branches of military service and consequently had age limitations. When a boy reached nineteen, he had to leave the brigade or join the territorial military force. Because Newfoundland had no senior military organization, apart from the Royal Navy Reserve, which had a limited roll of 600 at the time, there was no age

---

[7] PANL GN 238.

limitation. Newfoundland cadets were able to continue to serve in the brigades.

The St. John's CLB, a branch of the CLB's major body with headquarters in London, did have regulations regarding age limits. When a boy reached the age of nineteen, unless he held a non-commissioned rank, he had to leave the unit. The Church Lads Brigade in Newfoundland waived this rule because there was no senior organization into which the boy could graduate. Lt.-Col., Chief of Staff, W. Rendell of the Newfoundland Regiment, explained:

> The value of the boys' brigades has been more clearly demonstrated in Newfoundland than in any other part of the British Empire. Had it not been for these Brigades and the fairly efficient military training of their members, it is very doubtful whether Newfoundland would have raised its own distinctive regiment. Certainly, the first contingent could not have embarked for overseas in six weeks after the force was raised."[8]

The first contingent of the Regiment was brought up to battalion status and had a reserve to form a depot in June 1915. Rendell noted in a letter to Prime Minister Richard Squires in 1922, "It speaks well for the training of all ranks that within two months of that date, the battalion embarked for active service in Gallipoli."

Throughout the duration of the war, promotions in the non-commissioned and warrant ranks could be traced to the earlier boys' brigades training. About fifty percent of the 260 officers of the Newfoundland Regiment were originally trained in the boys' brigades. The boys' brigades in Newfoundland were entirely self-supporting and received no funding from the colonial government. The oldest of these brigades was the CLB.[9]

The Source of Designation "Caribou"

When the Newfoundland Regiment was formed in WWI, it adopted the Caribou insignia from the Methodist Highlanders as its

---

[8] PANL MG 439 Box 1 File 12, Department of Militia.
[9] Ibid.

Men who enlisted during WWI were trained in Pleasantville. (PANL)

own. The Highlanders Corps was founded in 1907 by Victor Gordon and it was styled after the St. Andrew's Presbyterian Boys' Brigade which was disbanded in the same year. The aim of the organization was to provide military training and discipline for young Newfoundlanders. They wore red tunics and kilts displaying the Gordon Highlander's Tartan. Instead of a summer camp, the Highlanders held an annual ten-day march from St. John's to Carbonear. Many of its members volunteered for service in World War I. The Methodist Highlanders organization was disbanded in 1924.[10]

Para-military Group Protected St. John's Harbour

At the outbreak of WWI, Newfoundland had a unique paramilitary organization operating on the island which was even stronger in Labrador. The Legion of Frontiersmen was made up of physical fit and militarily trained men, but due to lack of finances were lacking in guns and ammunition. Unlike the cadet corps, the Legionnaires trained men of military age.

The Frontiersmen was an organization founded in London, England, and in 1910 established its Newfoundland branch. The

---

[10] Jack Fitzgerald, <u>Fireside Stories</u>.

commanding officer for the Frontiersmen was Lieutenant Colonel D.P. Driscoll, DSO, a British war hero of the Boer War in South Africa, made famous by his role as the commanding officer of Driscoll's Scouts in that conflict.

The Legion of Frontiersmen was a non-sectarian organization with its required age for admission set at eighteen. It took root in the colony of Newfoundland because of its appeal to those who favoured the outdoor's life and the challenges of rigorous, physical activity. The Legion was particularly popular among the young men of Labrador.

Applicants were required to meet any one of three set conditions which included: (1) Being a veteran of war service; (2) experience at sea, or (3) experience in the wild. An applicant unable to meet any of the requirements had the choice of enrolling in the Legion's Auxiliary Force, provided he was of good character and eighteen years of age or older.

The first Newfoundland branch of the Frontiersmen was founded in 1910 in Battle Harbour, Labrador, by Dr. Arthur William Wakefield, a former Frontiersmen from England. St. John's born Mike Murphy, author, policeman, and newspaper editor, described the Frontiersmen as , "...an outfit to delight the hearts of Rudyard Kipling and Conan Doyle."

The appeal of adventure brought the Legion instant success in Newfoundland and Labrador where young men were experienced at sea and in the woods and were no strangers to handling a rifle. Wakefield quickly organized branches at Grand River, Mud Lake, St. Anthony, Nain, and Red Bay.

In 1912, he set up a branch in St. John's. The Frontiersmen had a popular drum and bugle band in the capital city that included regular drummers: Charlie Field, Walter Day, Albert Richards, Jimmy Adams and Sam Eddy, playing the bass drum; buglers were Jimmy Young, Jack Blyde, and Fred Andrews with Albert Fleming.

The Legion of Frontiersmen, with 150 members throughout Newfoundland and Labrador, was well established in Britain's oldest colony by August 1914 when war broke out. Wakefield felt that members of the Legion were physically fit and disciplined enough to fight for their country. He volunteered their service in a letter to Prime Minister Edward P. Morris. Wakefield wrote:

Our men in the North are mostly the picked men of the coast. They are the best hunters, the best shots, the hardiest, in a word, the best fighting stuff, and the men most capable of taking their place with credit along with the Frontiersmen from all over the world. Our force is organized, officered, drilled and uniformed, but poorly armed, as that has been an expense beyond our means.[11]

Wakefield was disappointed when Morris declined his offer, however, he encouraged members to enlist, and himself joined the Newfoundland Regiment and was sent overseas with the First Five Hundred in October 1914.

Dr. Arthur Wakefield volunteered as shooting instructor at the Southside Hills Rifle Range in St. John's and lived at the site while the troops were being trained. When it came time for him to go overseas with the Regiment, he made a rare and unusual offer to the Newfoundland Patriotic Association. He agreed to serve his entire active duty without pay. The only consideration he requested was that he be allowed to keep his field glasses, a compass, a revolver and the smallest Newfoundland gold piece obtainable. His request was granted.

When Dr. Wakefield entered the military, Vere Holloway succeeded him as commander of the Legion of Frontiersmen in Newfoundland. By July 15, 1915, seventy-two Frontiersmen had joined the Newfoundland Regiment and fourteen enlisted in the Royal Navy. Only six members remained active on the home front in St. John's. One of the first fatal casualties at Gallipoli, Turkey, in 1915 was Jack Blyde, a Frontiersman.

In England, Wakefield moved to the Royal Army Medical Corp. Most of the remaining Frontiersmen in Newfoundland enlisted in the Regiment or the Naval Reserve. Several dozen members kept up the organization in St. John's and took an active role in home defence.[12]

The story of the Frontiersmen was different in England. Due to the efforts of Colonel Driscoll, the Legion of Frontiersmen, there, was brought into the British Army. However, senior army

---

[11] Michael Murphy, Pathways to Yesteryear, Town Crier Publishing.
[12] At this time the organizing and financing of the military service was handled by the Newfoundland Patriotic Association.

officials were concerned because in their opinion the Legion members had not received proper discipline and training.

It was the influence of these officers that led to the decision to send the Legion to Africa where the type of warfare was more suitable to their training. They became the 25th Battalion (Frontiersmen) with 1166 members. The 25th Battalion was made up of an unusual assortment of men that included: ex-members of the French Foreign Legion, a circus clown, cowboys from Texas, miners from Australia and the Congo, pearl fishers, troopers from the North West Mounted Police, a lion tamer, music hall entertainers, an American millionaire and an ex-general of the Army of Honduras, who was dropped in rank to Sergeant in the 25th Battalion.

Author Mike Murphy noted that one member of the 25th Battalion was a person who had become well known in Newfoundland and was already a legendary figure in Africa. Murphy said, "He was none other than Frederick C. Selous, famous naturalist, explorer, and hunter, and friend of Teddy Roosevelt and Cecil Rhodes. He had been caribou hunting in Newfoundland on several occasions and loved the country."

Only one company of the 25th Battalion survived the battles fought in Africa. The others died in combat.

When the Legionaries assumed the responsibility for guarding the entrance to St. John's Harbour, there was concern over an enemy attack on the capital city.

No Submarine Defence in St. John's

Even a year after the Spring Rice Document, St. John's Harbour was still defenceless against a possible attack by a German submarine. In fact, according to the Commander-in Chief of North America and West Indies, Vice Admiral of the British Navy, George Patey, St. John's was without any defence whatsoever. Patey pointed out that this weakness in the colony's defence policy was reflected in Government's belief that if it was unable to provide a defence against enemy cruisers, it would be better to do nothing at all.

Patey warned:

This would be, to a certain extent justified in former times, but with the development of the submarine, the situation is altered. At present, it would be quite easy for one or two submarines armed with one or more guns to hold up the harbour and town of St. John's, take what they wanted and set fire and destroy the rest.[13]

The Vice-Admiral recommended that St. John's adopt a defence similar to that put in place by Halifax a year before. In June 1915, Halifax installed several anti-submarine nets at the entrance of its harbour. He said an added advantage would be to mount two twelve- pounder guns in appropriate places and to include the two three- pounder guns discarded by the *Calypso*, which were good for another 500 rounds of ammunition.

Commenting on the possibility of a German U-boat attack in Newfoundland waters, Patey stated, "I understand that the latest German submarines are easily capable of covering three to four thousand miles."[14]

It was under these circumstances that the Patriotic Association turned to the Legion of Frontiersmen to help fill the void.

The Legion of Frontiersmen received a boost in prestige on July 8, 1916, when four of their members were assigned to the Royal Newfoundland Regiment and were paid a salary by the Newfoundland Government. The four men: J. Hussey, Arthur Lucas, William Norris and Hayward Taylor, all with the rank of gunners, took over Waldegrave Battery near the entrance to St. John's harbour. They were stationed on the HMS *Briton*, moored near the Battery while construction work was being carried out on Fort Waldegrave overlooking Chain Rock.

Vere Holloway, a Lieutenant with the Newfoundland Regiment, was placed in charge with Sergeant E. Russell, his second in command. The Frontiersmen wore dark blue flannel shirts with patch pockets and brass buttons, a neckerchief, blue or khaki breeks and blue puttees. Their traditional Australian style slouch hats were replaced with seamen caps from the Royal Navy Reserve–bearing the name HMS *Briton*. In addition, they wore the Newfoundland Regiment shoulder badges displaying "NFLD." Lt. Holloway and Sgt. Russell wore forage caps displaying the badge of the Legion, a trumpet or bugle, similar to the badge of the Durham Light Infantry of the Imperial Army.

---

[13] PANL GN 1/3/A.
[14] Letter from Vice Admiral George Patey, June 3, 1915, to the Secretary of the Admiralty, Whitehall, London.

The four gunners moved into the Fort Waldegrave barracks when it was completed and slept in naval hammocks in "true naval fashion." At 6:00 a.m. daily the Sgt. Russell gave the order to "Rouse out and stow hammocks." Upon hearing this, the gunners jumped out of bed and stored their hammocks and bed coverings, then prepared for the day's assignments. Every day, with the exception of Sunday, was a busy day.

The daily routine at Fort Waldegrave centered around rifle drills and training in the use of the twelve-pounder gun which was the Fort's main defence. The twelve-pounder was a 1200 weight gun with the inscription stamped on the rear near the breech, "For Drill Only, 1900". Every member of the gun crew was supplied with a .303 rifle and Lt. Vere Holloway carried a revolver. They also worked at the building of an extension to their living quarters and on a stone wall around the fort.

The completed fort consisted of two powder magazines, one inside and one outside the fort. The main building contained living quarters for officers and men, a mess hall, and an office. The fort was surrounded by a stone wall which had two wooden gates seven or eight feet high.

In response to concerns over German submarine warfare, the Home Defence Committee had a boom installed at the entrance of St. John's harbour which went into operation on June 15. 1917. In addition, the harbour's leading lights and the lights at Fort Amherst were turned off and a blackout of the city enforced.

Discipline at Fort Waldegrave was as stern as in the regular military. Lt. Holloway was a strict disciplinarian who did not tolerate any nonsense from those under him when it came to any violations of the rules. Holloway presided over his first court-martial at Fort Waldegrave on September 3, 1916, less than three months after the command was set up. The prisoner, charged with drunkenness, was "summarily tried." A jury of three soldiers was appointed but the prisoner pleaded guilty. His punishment was the loss of "three general leaves" and a fine of five dollars.

Dismissal from the Legion of Frontiersmen was sometimes applied in situations where other branches of the military would have acted less severely. A gunner at the Battery who was charged with neglect of duty and disobedience was put in mufti (plain clothes) after his dismissal from service was ordered. Another gunner was reprimanded for "neglecting to wash himself clean."[15]

The boom and searchlights strengthened control of shipping entering and leaving the harbour. The boom stretched across the Narrows from Chain Rock from sunset to sunrise at which time it was lowered by the Frontiersmen.

Stationed near the boom on the outside was a motorboat with a mounted machine gun in its bow. The *Fiona*, a Newfoundland Government ship, was moored close by in position so that its searchlight commanded the Narrows. Upon the sighting of a vessel approaching the boom, when it was in raised position, the officer-in-charge of the steam launch would fire what was called a "very light", known today as a flare. This was the signal for the *Fiona*'s crew to switch on the searchlight. The Frontiersmen went on standby awaiting further instructions from the senior launch officer.

Fortunately, it was not necessary to fire on an approaching vessel. However, there was an occasion when the Frontiersmen came moments away from firing on a coastal boat that rammed through the boom. The captain on the *Fiona* recognized the vessel and instinctively signalled Fort Waldegrave to stand down just in time to stop the order "fire" from being given.

There are several versions of this episode, all conflicting. One has Lt. Vere Holloway being forcibly restrained by Sgt. Russell from taking over the gun to fire at the coastal boat. A factual account of what actually happened was not recorded in the Legion's log books. According to author Mike Murphy:

> The truth of the matter, according to a surviving member of the gun's crew, is that it was a hazy night with a storm brewing outside, and that made the coastal boat, under the command of Capt. Abram Kean, anxious to make port before the full fury of the storm broke. Kean himself a Skipper of the Royal Naval Reserve and not likely to break any rules regarding defence did, however, on this occasion forget or ignored the rules long enough to crash his ship through the boom defence. Lt. Vere Holloway, a stickler for the rules, was incensed at what he looked upon as a

---

[15] PANL MG 562 Box 1.

flagrant breach of the defence regulations and was all ready to give the signal to the gun's crew to take a pot shot at the coastal boat. But better judgement prevailed and Kean was allowed to proceed on course.

Hooligans became a problem around the Fort when under the cover of darkness, they stoned the living quarters. The unit's logbook noted,"On July 1, 1917, the sentry at Waldegrave challenged strangers about the Battery three times. No reply. Man started to run. Turned out guard. Searched hills and surrounding areas to no avail."

Tourists, mainly from the United States, enjoyed the scenery in the Signal Hill area where they visited to take pictures. The logbook recorded, "United States tourists with cameras watched with suspicion but did not use them." After a series of such entries, the Logbook noted, "Guard Lucas took American's camera and broke it and brought it to the fort. It was owned by an Edward Pullman Clarke." Three days later, a note in the Logbook stated, "American schooner leaving. Man fell overboard at 6:50 p.m. He was rescued by the *Harbour Pilot*." June 6, 1917.

On September 16, 1916 at 10:00 p.m., the sound of gunfire in the residential area of the Battery brought the Frontiersmen to an armed alert position. Everyone was relieved when it turned out to be a gun fired as part of a wedding celebration at the Battery.

A bit of a mystery was recorded in the logbook during June 1917. There were repeated sightings of two bright lights on the Southside Hills. The following night Sentry Lucas reported, "Strong white lights" on the Southside. These reports were passed on to the Constabulary. Lucas did report that it was a very dark night and a thunderstorm was expected.

A few weeks later a clothing supply was delivered to the Fort by the Newfoundland Regiment which included: three oilcoats (raincoats), three pairs rubber boots, two suits of underwear for each man, sixteen pairs of underwear all together.

On St. Patrick's Day, the Fort followed its usual holiday routine, which meant some rest and relaxation following a general cleaning up. Included in the jobs carried out by the Frontiersmen at the Fort was the building of a wall, excavation of rocks, drains, and the construction of several buildings.

All entries in the daily logbook were signed off by either the Lieutenant or the Sergeant, each using a code name which changed almost daily. The code names included: Cyclops, Marlborough, Rainbow, Russia, Centurion, Queen Elizabeth, Queen Mary, and Thunderer.

The names of guards appearing in the logbook included Hussey, Francis, Ludlow and Russell.[16]

The main building in the Fort was sold in 1920 and turned into a dance hall for people living in the area of the Battery and Signal Hill. According to the late Michael Cahill, who grew up at the Battery, after WWII it was converted into a family residence. By the late 1920s, declining interest led to the total abandonment of the Legion of Frontiersmen. Members of the organization made excellent soldiers and they contributed greatly to the war effort at home, at sea and on the battle fronts of Europe.

While other colonies and dominions were putting into operation their defence plans, Newfoundland, with no prior preparations or planning, responded rapidly. According to military historian G. W. Nicholson:

> The manner in which the authorities met the challenge and with the cooperation of the leading citizens (Newfoundland Patriotic Association) and the loyal support of practically the entire population of Newfoundland, efficiently organized and directed the country's military contribution to the forces of the Empire until the formation of a Department of Militia late in 1917, is without parallel under the British flag.[17]

Men who were not eligible to serve in the Regiment or the Navy Reserve were encouraged to enlist with the Foresters for service in the United Kingdom.

[16] PANL MG 562 Box 1.
[17] Ibid.

Chapter 4

"KICK 'EM TO BLUE BLAZES"

The call for volunteers to form a Newfoundland military was well received by the public, supported by the press, and even from the pulpit. Canon White, speaking during Sunday services at the Anglican Cathedral in St. John's, outlined the seriousness of what was happening in Europe and the need for Newfoundlanders to support the war effort. He concluded, "It is the duty of all Britishers to see this war through."

In Ferryland, on the Irish Loop along the southern shore of the Avalon Peninsula, the parish priest, Father Larry, was bruising in his endorsement of the call to arms. He told his congregation: "These Germans, shoot them! Go to the meeting and get ready to fight. Kick 'em to blue blazes," he concluded while performing a kicking motion.

Prime Minister Edward Morris was also strong in his appeal for volunteers for the new military force being organized. He said, "The colony should, if necessary, be prepared to give its last man and spend its last dollar in defence of the Empire."[1]

Royal Navy Reserve Volunteers preparing to leave St. John's Harbour-1914. (PANL)

---

[1] PANL M632 Box 1.

Newfoundland Regiment Volunteers leaving St. John's for overseas in 1915. (PANL)

When WWI broke out, Newfoundland had been almost fifty years without a military force. Raising an armed service from scratch presented major challenges. There was no question of Newfoundlanders loyalty to England, but there were problems and obstacles which needed to be overcome. For example, government quickly learned that mobilizing the Royal Navy Reserve during the fishing season was a major problem, and that was only the beginning of many challenges it had to face.

The will to stand at England's side was strong, and Governor Walter Davidson wasted no time in paving the way for a military in Newfoundland to join in its defence. With the approval of England's Secretary of State, the Governor initiated a plan to strengthen the naval reserve, land forces and initiate the training of men for home defence.

A preliminary meeting of prominent citizens and leaders led to the calling of a public meeting to set up a committee known as the Patriotic Association of Newfoundland (PAN). The meeting elected fifty men with Davidson as chairman. This organization took on the responsibility of increasing the size of the Royal Navy Reserve (RNR) to train men for the Royal Navy, as well as, the raising of a full regiment of volunteers to fight in Europe. The first proclamation calling for volunteers for the land forces was issued on August 21, 1914. The PAN's work involved the raising, equipping, transporting and the caring for the land contingents for three years. The PAN, in effect, served as Newfoundland's War Department in directing the Colony's war effort. At the end of the three year period, its responsibilities were to be taken over by the Department of Militia.

By 1917, when a Government Department of Militia was set up, the PAN had raised and was financing two Battalions in the war. Governor Davidson by-passed the elected Government to do this because he felt that the politics of the day would drag down any war effort in petty squabbling.

Loyalty to Britain was strong throughout its oldest colony, and the appeal to join the cause on the battlefronts of Europe was heard loud and clear. In just sixty days, Newfoundland had raised a full regiment. In doing so, the colony least prepared became the first among the colonies to come to Britain's aid with a military force. The war was anticipated to last about one year, but it became apparent that this would not be the case. While the First Five Hundred were still in training, the call went out for additional volunteers.

St. John's Training Locations

Two sites were selected to accommodate the new regiment and to provide for its training. The old cricket pitch in Pleasantville adjacent to Quidi Vidi Lake with its beautiful meadows and countryside became a tent city to house the regiment. However, severe wind and rainstorms caused havoc with the site in its first weeks when forty tents were either damaged or destroyed. This unexpected experience proved valuable to the men later in Gallipoli. A shelter that could house 150 men was quickly constructed at a cost of $200. The land in Pleasantville was provided rent free by its owner a Mr. Woodley. Businessman John Clouston provided the use of four cooking ranges free of charge.

All lumbermen and skilled workers who were not eligible for the Regiment or the RNR were invited to enlist in the Foresters for service in the United Kingdom. The response was slow at first but men from all over the Colony including St. John's stepped forward to volunteer.

The rifle range on the Southside Hills was transformed from a site used only for shooting practice and competitions to include a small training base which handled fifty regimental recruits at a

Newfoundland Regiment members training at Pleasantville during September 1914. (PANL)

Newfoundland Regiment Training Camp at Pleasantville adjacent to Quidi Vidi Lake. (PANL)

time. Shelters were built to house and feed these men during their training. The PAN put together a team of forty expert marksmen to train the soldiers at the rifle range. The instructors were from St. John's and nearby communities, and most were involved in the various cadet corps and rifle clubs around the city. Soldiers who could not use the rifle after training were discharged. A total of twenty-one men fell into that category. On September 12th a rifle competition was held between the Royal Navy Reserve and the Newfoundland Regiment recruits; the Regiment defeated the Navy Reserves by a score of 538 to 500.

Catholic members of the Blue Puttee were marched to this Roman Catholic Church in Ayr on St. Patrick's Day in 1915 led by Major Peter Cashin. (Paul Sweeney)

By September 19th 500 Ross Rifles and 100 Lee Enfield Rifles had been received from Canada. Surplus revolvers on hand were sold in England.[2]

By the time their training ended and uniforms were issued, the First Five Hundred to go overseas were now known as the Blue Puttees, a name immortalized in the colony's wartime history.

The problems in finding appropriate military uniforms led to the necessity of using blue instead of khaki puttees. The blue puttees were extra supplies owned by the Church Lads Brigade who gladly contributed them to the new Regiment. T. Andrews writing in *Forgotten Heroes* stated:

> Newfoundland had no stocks of uniforms available and the London War Office was unable to furnish any of the material with which to make them. Canada could only supply greatcoats. Consequently, local manufacturers were

---

[2] Ibid.

Members of the Blue Puttees, (1st 500) leaving St. John's on the Florizel. (PANL)

Blue Puttees on the Florizel. There was a shortage of hats when the first five hundred disembarked for England in 1915. (PANL)

commissioned to produce fatigue uniforms. Groundsheet, blankets, shorts, socks, underwear and boots were purchased on local tender. Since no Khaki material was available to make puttees, the troops were issued puttees of navy blue. The only Newfoundlanders to wear these were those who formed the first contingent to leave St. John's in October, 1914, and the unusual garb was to become a badge of honour. To be a 'Blue Puttee' was to be a member o of the renowned First Five Hundred.[3]

The Blue Puttees left St. John's on October 4, 1914. There was an adventurous mood among the new recruits who enthusiastically

---

[3] The Legion of Frontiersmen also wore blue puttees which were donated to them by the CLB. However, only the overseas force to use these were the First Five Hundred.

em-braced the opportunity to get a break from the monotony of everyday life. However, many may have had their spirits dampened aboard the SS *Florizel* as it passed out the Narrows of St. John's Harbour carrying them to England. Conditions aboard ship quickly dampened the mood that had previously been experienced among the recruits.

Lt. A. W. Wakefield recalled later, "Men's accommodation for sleeping, messing, washing and latrines were ridiculously insufficient. Food arrangements were disgraceful."[4]

The Scots Embrace Newfoundland Regiment

In the first weeks after their arrival in the United Kingdom, the question of whether the Blue Puttees would become part of an established unit or operate as an independent Newfoundland unit remained undecided. Some among the recruits were concerned that they might lose their identity if they were incorporated into one of the Canadian units. Captain J. Fox explained:

> We felt, quite properly, that if we were to give our best, we could only do so by preserving our own individuality. There was the fear that our identity would be lost with some Canadian unit. Not that we had developed a "superiority complex" so far as our neighbours were concerned."[5]

It didn't help the situation when they were greeted by a Highland Band playing "The Maple Leaf Forever". It did not take long for the Blue Puttees to let the Scots know that they were not Canadian and what they wanted to hear was the Newfoundland Regimental march, "The Banks of Newfoundland". The Scots went out of their way to oblige the Newfoundlanders. They not only came up with music sheets for the march, but also put together an assortment of Newfoundland music which lifted the spirits of the Newfoundlanders. By this time, the Regiment had been reinforced to full battalion strength of about 1200 officers and men. When the Newfoundland and the Scots soldiers welcomed in the New Year 1915 at Edinburgh Castle, the Regiment Band and the Scots

---

[4] Facey-Crowther, <u>Better Than the Best</u>. 1995.
[5] <u>Veteran's Magazine</u>, 1928 CNS.

Members of the Newfoundland Regiment were housed at the Newton Park school, Ayr, Scotland in 1915. They were later moved to the Horse Racing Course at Ayr. (PANL)

Pipers were a big hit as they performed both Scottish and Newfoundland music.

The Regiment spent ten months in Scotland undergoing heavy training at Salisbury Plain, Fort George near Inverness, Stobs Camp near Harwick, and Aldershot.

The first prestigious honour received by the Newfoundland Regiment in Europe during WWI was to become the first overseas troops to be conferred with the guardianship of the historic Edinburgh Castle also known in Scotland as "Auld Reeke." The Newfoundlanders are also the only non-Scottish troops ever to be garrisoned in the castle.[6]

It is an honour still remembered in Scotland by a commemorative plaque inside the castle, which was placed there in 1954 by the Royal Canadian Legion. Private J. Ryan of St. John's recalled, "We were always welcome in the Highlands as being the first colonial troops to enter Scotland."[7]

Scots Welcomed Blue Puttees

The population of Edinburgh developed an admiration and a fond relationship with members of the Newfoundland Regiment

---

[6] G.W. Nicholson, The Fighting Newfoundlander.
[7] Facey-Crowther, Better Than the Best, 1995, p30.

stationed at Edinburgh Castle. Even senior British officers gave preferential treatment to the Newfoundlanders. In a letter to Governor Walter Davidson, Major Whitaker pointed out that while the Royal Engineers were still waiting on the arrival of much needed equipment, the Newfoundland Regiment had plenty of picks, shovels, and barbed wire, all of which were needed by the Engineers. The Newfoundland Regiment was also assigned the best instructors.

Although, at first, their presence took a little getting used to, many a townsman, passing by the Castle at night, was taken aback to witness one or two Newfoundland soldier sliding down a rope or blanket from a window in the castle in order to go out on the town. David Carew, from 33 Patrick Street was stationed at the castle, and after leaving it one night, by way of rope, did not return for two days. When he returned, he was given three days in the brig. Less than a year later on October 7, 1915, Carew was shot by a sniper at Gallipoli.

Newfoundlanders popularity increased when it became known around Edinburgh that the Regiment had the only bar in town that was opened on Sundays.

The Beginning of the Regiment Band

The formation of The Royal Newfoundland Regiment Band is an interesting part of the regiment's history. It was formed in Scotland while the Regiment was in training during January 1916.

Newfoundland Regiment Band playing at Edinburgh Castle in 1915. (PANL)

The Newfoundland Regimental Band marching to the 3rd London General Hospital September 1917 for a special performance for wounded soldiers. This was part of the Newfoundland Week celebrations in London. The Regiment's Mascot Sable Chief leads the way. (IWM)

Prior to and during this period marching music for the soldiers was supplied by the Regiment's bugle and drum band.[8]

In the previous year, Sir Edgar Bowring and several unnamed contributors had donated a complete set of instruments to the Regiment. Soldiers took some of these instruments with them to Gallipoli and others were held in storage while the Regiment completed its training program. During a battle with the Turks after their arrival in Suvla Bay, a Turkish shell struck the hiding place where the instruments were stored and destroyed them.[9]

The first step in organizing the band was to find a capable bandmaster. One was found in L.L. Worthington, an experienced bandmaster, who proceeded to organize and lead the first Newfoundland Regiment Band. Worthington had served as bandmaster with the 1st Battalion, King's (Liverpool) Regiment and

---

[8] MG 438.
[9] PANL GN-1/3/A. Historian G.W. Nicholson's says the Regiment lost its bugle and drum band's instruments, but makes no mention of the brass band instruments. The Fighting Newfoundlander. G.W. Nicholson, p171.

Sable Chief resting between performances during Newfoundland Week in London during September 1917. Lady Morris looks on in admiration. Sir Edward Morris is second from right. Sable Chief was trained to stand at attention while the Regimental march The Banks of Newfoundland was played. (PANL)

after leaving the military, became bandmaster of the Ayr Burgh Band of Scotland. To entice him out of retirement, he was made a Warrant Officer, First Class, with the Newfoundland Regiment. He brought with him several of his old players whom he added to the Regiment's existing buglers and drummers to form the new band.

It did not take long for the new band to accompany the troops on marches as well as concerts and other entertainment. On St. Patrick's Day, 1916, Lieutenants Peter Cashin and Leo Murphy led 150 (Catholic) members of the Regiment to St. Margaret's Church in Ayr to attend mass.

Citizens of the community lined the streets and delighted in its music. The next day a local newspaper reported, "The band rendered gems of Irish music along the route of march and all the troops wore the Irish emblem, the shamrocks, which were presents from Dublin."[10]

---

[10] Ibid.

The Regimental band was given the honour of leading all overseas forces in the parade for the historic annual Lord Mayor of London's Parade and Pageant on November 9, 1916. This honour was reserved by right of seniority for the band and regiment from Newfoundland, the oldest colony. Most of these were veterans of Gallipoli or the Somme, and bore on their sleeve the famous red triangle badge of the 29th Division of which they were members.

Thousands of Londoners lining the route applauded long and loudly for the Newfoundlanders and their band. As they passed the Law Courts, the Lord Mayor took the salute and the band struck up, "The Banks of Newfoundland". Later in the parade, they played the same music while passing the Lord Mayor's Mansion.[11]

In 1917, to pay honour and tribute to the courage and battlefront conduct of the Newfoundland Regiment, the British celebrated the 420th anniversary of the discovery of Newfoundland by holding a Newfoundland week. An editorial in the *London Times* paid tribute to the oldest colony's performance in war. It read, "Can a small, remote, and comparatively poor community like this act in a way that will stimulate the whole spirit of Empire? The deeds of the Newfoundlanders show that it can."

Unfortunately, most Newfoundlanders could not attend the celebrations because the 1st Battalion of Newfoundlanders was in Flanders, France and the 2nd (Reserve) Battalion was training in Scotland. However, guests were welcomed from the administrative staff of both Regiments and special arrangements were made to include the wounded and the Regimental Band.

On September 22nd, the Regimental Band was brought to London from Ayr and gave a concert in Hyde Park attended by 10,000 people. This was followed by two concerts daily for the remainder of the week. Included in their program was a performance on the grounds of the London General Hospital where 1500 wounded Newfoundlanders were being treated. Traffic jams occurred outside where busses and cars stopped to listen to some of the familiar strains performed including, "If you were the only girl in the world."

The highlight of the tour was the performance at His Majesty's Theatre in London in aid of the British Red Cross Society's

---

[11] G.W. Nicholson, <u>The Fighting Newfoundlander</u>, p324.

Prisoners of War Fund. The Regiment's mascot which was Sable Chief, a Newfoundland Dog, was there with a collection box tied to his neck. Sable Chief went wherever the Band performed. He was even trained to stand at attention when "The Banks of Newfoundland" was played.

The Band's last performance before returning to Scotland was at Buckingham Palace which was attended by His Majesty King George V. The Queen and Princess Mary watched from a window in the Palace. King George awarded Bandmaster Worthington the medal of the Royal Victorian Order on behalf of the Newfoundland Regimental Band, and complimented the band members on their fine performance. *The Daily Mail*'s music critic reported next day, "This body of thirty picked players is more than able to hold its own with military bands with far greater resources." He compared "The Banks of Newfoundland" to the British marching tune "Sir Roger de Coverley", with perhaps even more spring in it.

Not all comments were as complimentary. According to military historian, G. Nicholson, one newspaper said, "London heard the curious march of the Regiment, a mixture of Irish and Red Indian strains, as stirring as it is weird."

Awakened by "Banks of Newfoundland"

On March 5, 1917, the Newfoundland Regiment arrived for two weeks stay in the divisional reserve at Meaulte, France, a tiny village between Ville-sous-Corbie and Albert. Millions of soldiers had passed through its main street since the start of the war. Unknown to the Newfoundland soldiers, the Regimental Band had arrived in France a few days earlier. At about 7:30 one morning, the band drove into the village in an old military truck. The Regiment had returned from the battlefront the previous night and were fast asleep in their billets.

Bandmaster, L.L. Worthington, decided to give his fellow soldiers a surprise. He loaded the band aboard a truck and drove slowly through the streets playing a series of military tunes, but received no results. It didn't work, and the quiet village remained silent. An idea struck him, one that he felt was sure to get any Newfoundlander moving under the circumstances. He called upon the band to play "The Banks of Newfoundland". The result was magical.

Instantly, doors and windows swung open and out through them came Newfoundland soldiers partially clad and dragging their clothes with them. The music kept up until there was a full turn out and they all marched off to breakfast.[12]

"The Banks of Newfoundland" was arranged as a stirring march by Worthington and adopted as the official Regimental March. Its history goes back to 1819 when it was written by Sir Francis Forbes, Chief Justice of Newfoundland, while on a ship sailing on the Grand Banks.

It was first played in public by an Irish Piper at a dinner of the Benevolent Irish Society held on St. Paddy's Day, 1820. Historian Nicholson said, "This stirring tune came to serve as a lasting memorial to the famous Regiment whose troops rallied to its historic and stimulating strains."

The band played at the 1917 St. Paddy's Eve concert in the YMCA Hut at Meaulte. The hall was filled to capacity and the event remained in the minds of the soldiers for decades afterwards. Prime Minister Sir Edward Morris and Sir Edgar Bowring were in attendance and Morris, known for his oratory, had the audience roaring in laughter over the anecdotes he recalled from home.

The "Mayo Lind Tobacco Fund"

Newfoundlanders at home were kept informed of the Regiment at war through letters some of the troops sent to the local newspapers. One of these letters from the battlefront made the name of Private Frank 'Mayo' Lind famous throughout Newfoundland. How Lind got the nickname "Mayo" is one of the fascinating anecdotes of the Newfoundland Regiment in WWI. Lind was born at Betts Cove, Newfoundland, in 1879 and was educated at Little Bay. His letters from the battlefront to the *Daily News* inspired the organization of the "Mayo Lind Tobacco Fund," set up to keep the troops supplied with tobacco.

Lind was employed as a clerk in Fogo when the war broke out. He was one of the first volunteers from the area to enlist in the Newfoundland Regiment. His regular correspondence to the *Daily News* became very popular. He described the living conditions, the spirit of the men and the challenges being faced... The letter which made him a celebrity at home and among members of the

[12] Ibid.

Regiment was written by him from Gallipoli on May 20, 1915. In it he mentioned a need which resonated with the general public– a stick of Mayo. He wrote, "It is almost impossible to get good tobacco in this country, a stick of Mayo is indeed a luxury."

The newspaper office was overwhelmed with donations to buy tobacco for "our troops over there." The Imperial Tobacco Company, makers of Mayo plug, teamed up with the *Daily News* in setting up a fund to purchase tobacco for the troops. The project rapidly became known as "The 'Mayo' Lind Tobacco Fund."[13]

The Newfoundland Government supported the fund by waiving import and excise duties on tobacco donated to the troops. This concession helped the Mayo Lind Committee to send monthly to each man: a half pound of plug tobacco; forty cigarettes and a box of matches. The Imperial Tobacco Company packaged and shipped the parcels without any charge to the fund. Newfoundlanders serving with the Royal Navy were included in the mailing list.

Lind continued his letters to the *Daily News*, recording the hardships of the Battle at Gallipoli, his recuperation from wounds at Malta, and the transfer of the Regiment to France. His last letter was written the evening before his death on July 1, 1916, at Beaumont Hamel, France. He wrote:

> We are out to billets again for a short rest, returning to the trenches tomorrow and then– never mind that now. Tell everybody that they may feel proud of the Newfoundland Regiment for we get nothing but praise from the Divisional General down.[14]

The *Daily News* continued to sponsor the Mayo Lind Tobacco Fund until the end of the war when they published a booklet titled *32 Letters of Mayo Lind*.

Menu & Sanitary Conditions

The everyday routine of regularly prepared meals and a good supply of drinking water evident in the training camps at Scotland was in stark contrast to battlefield practices on the Gallipoli

---

[13] Joseph R. Smallwood, <u>Encyclopaedia of Newfoundland and Labrador.</u>
[14] Ibid.

battlefront. Hardtack and tea were frequently supplied, and, when possible, the men were given bacon with the hardtack. The evening meal, or 'tea-time' as the British and Newfoundlanders called it, was simple. It was comprised of hard biscuit, the type used to make fish and brewis, with cheese or jam, and a cup of hot tea. 'Rissoles' were a treat. These were made by mixing crumbs and bully beef together and frying it in margarine or bacon fat when it was available. These had to be eaten hot, but if cold, the soldiers pushed them aside.

In Gallipoli, drinking water was scarce and the men were frequently rationed to one half-pint daily. The few wells near the trenches were contaminated and soldiers had to be cautious in selecting water for drinking.

The mornings were spent in the care and maintenance of the trenches. By mid-day, this chore would be finished and the soldiers would have to deal with the reality of the unavoidable unsanitary conditions of trench life. The trenches were infested with the "Suvla Plain lice" which took up residence in their shirts and blankets. The men took time to patiently pick these lice from their shirts, which gave them a few hours comfort before the unwelcomed tenants again took over. At night, the lice were there to torment the men and keep them awake. Swimming and washing clothing in nearby Suvla Bay helped, but in itself was very hazardous due to the constant risk of an artillery attack.

Why Newfoundlanders Were Sent to Gallipoli

The motive behind the offensive to force the Dardanelles was to provide Russia, an ally, with access to the Mediterranean. The Dardanelles is the Strait between the Aegean Sea and the Sea of Marmara that separates Europe from Turkey. The Strait is also referred to as the Hellespont. Gallipoli is on the Turkish side and the bay at the mouth of the strait is Suvla Bay. It was on the beaches of Suvla Bay that the Royal Newfoundland Regiment, as part of the British forces landed in 1915. The offensive started on October 3, 1914, while the Newfoundland Regiment was still in training, when the navies of Britain and France launched a heavy bombardment of the Turkish Forts at the entrance to the Dardanelles Straits. A second assault on the area was launched on February 19, 1915, which confirmed enemy suspicions that the Allies strategy was to break through the Dardanelles.

This sparked an intense response from the Turks who initiated massive actions to fortify the entire length of the Straits. The British led forces (Allies) continued the bombardment throughout March in a futile effort that cost them great losses in men and ships. The allied generals reconsidered their strategy and concluded that only a combined land and sea effort could win the offensive. However, a land assault presented some major challenges due to what was described by some as, "...an inhospitable shore." Obstacles included the need to provide water over long distance; and the lack of fortified harbours where ships could secure rest and refit and where troops could take much needed rest.[15]

On April 25, 1915, England landed 75,000 troops at Cape Helles on the tip of the Gallipoli Peninsula. This was the beginning of the offensive to open the Dardanelles. Despite their successful landings, the Allies were unable to utilize them to their advantage.[16]

Regardless of these major difficulties, the Allies moved forward by sending 120,000 troops. Part of this first land offensive was the 29th Division which fought an epic battle on the beaches at Cape Helles. After three months of battling, strategists came up with another plan to break the deadlock. They decided to land troops at Suvla Bay and seize the adjacent heights.

A serious error was made by the General in charge who had delayed forty-eight hours in moving the troops ahead to take up positions. The Turks (part of the German led Central Powers) used this time to move up all their available equipment and forces to take up gun positions which gave them a major advantage over the Allied troops' advance.

At this stage, General de Lisle took command of the Allied troops and led the advance. However, they were stopped dead in their tracks a few thousand yards from the water's edge. The 5th Royal Scots, one of the units of the 88th Brigade of the 29th Division was decimated and unable to continue as a fighting unit. It was at this time, that the Newfoundland Regiment arrived at Suvla Bay, in time to fill the gap in the 88th Brigade left by the decimation of the Royal Scots. The survivors of the Royal Scots were added to the

---

[15] PANL MG 438.

[16] George Ferrell, general editor, Twentieth Century Almanac.

Newfoundland Regiment to form the Newfoundland Battalion of the 88th Brigade.

The Newfoundland Regiment had departed for Gallipoli on August 20, 1915, on the S.S. *Megantic*. They disembarked at Alexandria, Egypt on September 1st, and, following a short stay, they continued on to Gallipoli where they landed on the beach at Suvla on the evening of September 19th.

The Newfoundland Regiment got their first taste of war the day after their arrival when they were bombarded by enemy fire. They handled it like the professional soldiers they had become. Small platoons dodged the shells to move successfully towards trenches four miles away at Sari Bair.

Major General D.E. Cayley was in charge of the 88th Brigade when the Newfoundlanders arrived at Suvla. He was impressed by the condition of the Blue Puttees as they set foot on the shores of Gallipoli. Cayley noted in a letter after the war to officials in Newfoundland, "When I first saw the Regiment behind the line at Suvla, I was immediately struck by the physique of the men, not on the whole very tall, but unusually sturdy and stocky."[17]

He added that they displayed a very high standard of discipline and routine.

Prior to the Newfoundlanders' arrival, the 88th Brigade and the New Zealanders Regiment had captured Sari Bair, a strategic hill, not far from Suvla Beach. However, the relief troops that succeeded them were unable to hold the position and the Turks reclaimed the hill. The 88th Brigade dug in and held the trenches at the foot of Sari Bair until they were joined by the Newfoundlanders on September 20th.[18]

The Turks attempted to take the trenches on September 28th, but their efforts were unsuccessful. They were at a disadvantage. In order to get to Allied trenches, they had to go over the crest of a ridge that was 700 yards away and within the firing range of the Suvla batteries. Each time the Turks attempted to climb the ridge, they were shelled by ships laying in the harbour and artillery fire from the Suvla batteries.

---

[17] PANL MG 439 Box 1.
[18] G.W. Nicholson, The Fighting Newfoundlander.

Blue Puttees Deceive the Turks

A patrol of three, led by J. L. Donnelly, became pinned down by the Turks on one of those nightly patrols. The unit made it to a ridge located midway between the enemy positions on top of the hill and the Newfoundland trenches below. The Newfoundlanders were outnumbered seven to one by the attacking force but were able to hold them off.

A rescue group of six men, led by Lieutenant H. Ross and Sergeant Greene, were sent to support Donnelly's patrol. The rescuers set out in darkness and, when they were challenged by someone shouting "Who goes there?" Ross answered, "Newfoundlanders." This answer was followed by shouting with only two words coming across clearly to Ross. These were "Newfoundlanders!" and "Allah!" Gunfire erupted immediately. Ross's patrol had encountered a Turkish unit which was attempting to surround Donnelly's Patrol. A Private James Ellsworth was killed during the scrimmage. The Blue Puttees put up such a display of machine gun firing that the Turks, thinking they were facing a much larger opposition, retreated.

Donnelly's patrol held the ridge until next morning when the Regiment advanced and took control. For the remainder of their stay in Gallipoli, there were no major offensives launched by the Turks. For his part in this battle, Donnelly was awarded the Military Cross. Each of the two others with him, Sgt. W. Green and Pte. R. Hynes, won the Distinguished Conduct Medal. Lance Corporal Fred Snow was awarded the Military Medal. This ridge was named Caribou Hill in honour of the Newfoundlanders.[19]

Another soldier honoured at Gallipoli, soon after, was Pte. William J. Gladney of Portugal Cove who was awarded the Distinguished Conduct Medal. Gladney, manoeuvring independently, came within five yards of the Turkish trenches. He located four machine guns, shot two sentries and brought back valuable intelligence to his senior officer. His heroic story is told in a later chapter.

---

[19] PANL GN 1/10 "Newfoundland Forces in World War I, Records of the Royal Newfoundland Regiment." H.M. Mosdell, M.S., <u>What Year was That?</u>

The Fighting Carew Brothers. Four Carew brothers fought with the Blue Puttees at Gallipoli. David, was shot at Gallipoli, John was killed during the Battle of Beaumont Hamel. William and Thomas survived the war. L-R: Privates: John Carew, William Carew, and David Carew Missing from photo is Thomas Carew. (Courtesy of Owen and Jean (Carew) Moore)

Unsuspected Enemy Strikes

After the Turks retreated, the trenches became the Newfoundlanders' front line. They were about to confront a new enemy. Over the next two months they learned that there was more to fear in war than enemy bullets.

The Turks had retreated to the top of the nearby hill, and the land separating them from the Newfoundlanders became a no-man's-land. Each side held the other pinned down, and neither side could advance, nor could they remove their dead comrades who were rotting in the field separating them.

The winds, gently sweeping across no-man's-land, carried germs from the putrefied corpses into the trenches, contaminating the food supplies, and spreading disease when inhaled by its occupants. An epidemic of Enteric Fever, a form of typhoid marked by intestinal inflamation and ulceration, broke out. In addition, dysentery rapidly spread among the soldiers. Their suffering was worsened when enemy snipers detected where their water supplies were hidden and made it almost impossible for the Blue Puttees to access the water.

Among the Newfoundlanders in the trenches were three brothers, John, David and William Carew from 35 Patrick Street, St. John's. After a period of being pinned down, Private David Carew attempted to stretch, but when his head appeared above the parapet, a sniper fired, hitting Carew in the head and killing him instantly. His two brothers, John and William, dug a grave to bury him.

Prior to their departure from Newfoundland, all ranks had been given the full program of protective immunization. There were so many needles given that a private from Carbonear wrote to his mother, "Don't fret about my being sick. I have three or four doses of inoculation and four of vaccinations, so if all the Turks start to decay at the same time, they won't affect me."[20]

The Great Storm

The Newfoundlanders had arrived in Gallipoli well prepared for battle. They were among the best physically fit men in the 29th Division. The Blue Puttees easily handled digging trenches, carrying sixty to seventy pound haversacks over long distances, dodging bullets and even carrying out nighttime penetrations behind enemy lines. Yet there was something they were not prepared for, nor had given much thought to, – the Gallipoli weather,– unpredictable, fierce, violent, and long lasting storms.

They had paid little attention to the gale force winds blowing along the coast of Gallipoli in early November. These were not harmless winds because they destroyed shipping and beach installations along the coast from Helles to Suvla. The troops were more focussed on fighting Turks than worrying about windstorms. Yet, after all, they had come from Newfoundland, an island in the North Atlantic, which some visitors have described as, "The only place on earth where all four winds blow at the same time."

As the month of November slipped by and the winds slowly intensified, the Newfoundlanders held their position on the battlefront. With the combat experience they were gathering, they were ready for almost anything. But, a "Storm" more destructive and terrifying than armed combat was creeping up on them unnoticed, and they were not the least prepared to confront it when it struck.

---

[20] G.W. Nicholson, The Fighting Newfoundlander.

It hit with vengeance on November 26th, and, by the time it ended, the experience had become embedded into the minds of every soldier present. Even decades later, when veterans recalled Gallipoli, it was this that they remembered most – "The Great Storm!" Not even the Turks could handle it!

On November 26, 1915, menacing clouds darkened the early morning skies, and then it seemed like the sky just broke open. It started with a torrential rainfall, deafening thunder and blinding lightning accompanied by hurricane force winds. Temperatures dropped, the rain turned into sleet and then a blizzard. The trenches, the battlefront home for the Blue Puttees, were turned into rivers until their walls could not retain the force any longer, and they began collapsing like dominoes falling across the front.

Ironically, the shipment of winter clothing received earlier in the week had been sent back the day before because the decision had been made to evacuate all Allied soldiers from the Gallipoli Peninsula. One soldier wrote home, "As the swirling, freezing waters passed over me, I had to unstrap my gun and let her go."[21]

Another Blue Puttee, Private F. LeGrow, remembered:

When the big storm came in Gallipoli, I was lying in a dugout with my head towards a fire. The next morning my boots were frozen in the mud and I had to take them off to get my feet free. My feet were frost bitten and I spent a year in Hospital. It would have been better if I had put my feet near the fire to save them from frostbite. A soldier doesn't need to use his head, but his feet are most important.[22]

The suffering of the Blue Puttees was dreadful. In the trenches where troops sought refuge, they were waist-deep in water. Things worsened during the night when temperatures dropped and the rain turned into sleet accompanied by a biting north wind. On November 28th, the weather further deteriorated. Temperatures dropped even lower; the winds became colder and a blinding snowstorm struck. When the storm finally ended, the 29th Division had lost two-thirds of its men. However, not one Newfoundlander was among them. One hundred and fifty Newfoundlanders, mostly

---

[21] PANL GN- 1/10, Newfoundland Forces in World War I.
[22] Dr. David Facey-Crowther, Better Than the Best.

with frostbitten feet, were hospitalized. Fortunately, the day before the storm hit, forty-one of the sick and injured had been evacuated.

Many men continued to perform duties during the struggle for survival in the lengthy storm. Unable to get their swollen, frostbitten feet into their footwear, they filled sandbags with straw, rubbed their feet with whale oil and used the bags as footwear. Frostbite was rampant and there were many amputations due to gangrene setting in.

The uselessness of the Dardanelles Offensive was apparent when General Sir Charles Monroe planned and directed the evacuation of the entire Gallipoli Peninsula. This was a daring and challenging strategy with great risk in which the Newfoundland Regiment played a shining role. Approximately 60,000 troops and most of their equipment were withdrawn right under the nose of the enemy without a man being lost.

The Blue Puttees put up an admirable and memorable display of ingenuity and courage when it came time to evacuate the troops from Gallipoli. The 88th Brigade was assigned the full responsibility to hold the entire divisional front stretching 3,000 yards while the remainder of the 29th Division was being evacuated. On the last night of evacuation, all the front trenches were covered by forty men from each of the Battalions of the 88th, left alone to provide cover until all others were safely evacuated.[23]

After the storm ended, the battalion moved to Cape Helles, on the Gallipoli Peninsula where they arrived on December 24th. To help regain their focus after the nightmare at Gallipoli, the Newfoundlanders became very active. They undertook the construction of roads and bridges, and later, built piers and loaded material onto ships in preparation for the evacuation of Cape Helles. The stay was a short one and on January 9th, after the departure of several parties, the remainder of the Newfoundland Regiment acted as a rearguard for the last troops to leave Cape Helles.

One Naval Reservists Experience at Dardanelles

Nath Somerton of Portugal Cove was among the 200 members of the Royal Navy Reserve in Newfoundland who left for Gallipoli on the SS *Mongolian* in February 1915. First, however, the

---

[23] PANL MG 439 Box 1.

vessel had to get them to Halifax to pick up other volunteers, but it began to leak. The new sailors succeeded in getting the ship safely to Halifax where they were transferred to the troopship *Scandinavian* and were delivered without incident to England.

In London, the Newfoundlanders were split up and assigned to different ships in the British Navy. Somerton was assigned to the minesweeper *Supporter* where he was promoted to Gunner and placed in charge of the ammunition and rifles. His ship remained on patrol in the English Channel until May 1915 when they were ordered to the Dardanelles.

They evaded Turkish shells from land while assisting English and Australian troops in landing on the beach at Anzac on the Gallipoli Peninsula. Somerton's ship would carry 200 men at a time from their transport ship to within a half mile from shore, dodging enemy artillery fire all the way. At that point, their passengers were transferred to small launches and open boats which conveyed them to land.

In one delivery, they were attacked by rifles from shore which swept the *Supporter's* decks killing twenty-five men in one attack. Despite the heavy losses occurring in the landings, Somerton escaped injury. His ship continued to land troops successfully over the subsequent two months. While in the Dardanelles and Gallipoli area, the *Supporter* had many close encounters at it used anti-sub nets to sweep mines and deliver munitions to the men fighting in Gallipoli.

When leaving the Dardanelles for England, they encountered a raging December storm on the coast of Greece. While scanning the horizon, the Captain caught sight of a group of men waving from nearby land. It was far too rough to make a rescue by landing there. Somerton later told reporters that the *Supporter* did make an unsuccessful attempt to land a lifeboat to help them but the heavy sea forced it back. He explained, "Owing to the heavy sea, the boat we launched could not be rowed to land, so we put out a guide rope with an anchor attached which the shipwrecked men used in turn to get on board our patrol boat. There were sixty of them."

It turned out that these shipwrecked sailors were from two Italian merchant vessels torpedoed earlier that week by a German U-boat. Eighteen of their countrymen went down with their ships. When Somerton returned home to Portugal Cove during July

1916, he remained in the Royal Navy Reserve and served on the HMS *Briton*.

By the time the Gallipoli Campaign ended, the Allied Forces had suffered over 5000 casualties. Trench life at Gallipoli was far more severe than what they experienced anywhere else in the war.

The authors of the book *Marching to Armageddon* said that the main reason for the failure in Gallipoli was the shortage of artillery shells. In March 1915, field artillery guns were rationed to eight rounds a day. In April, the ration was increased to ten rounds. When word of this reached the British public it caused an outrage that forced Prime Minister Asquith into a coalition with the Conservatives. Britains munitions industry could not meet the demands of war and the British turned to Canada which by 1917 had 600 munition factories.

Winston Churchill, on the other hand, attributed the failure to Lord of the Admiralty, Sir Herbert Kitchener's failure to follow the original plan agreed upon by the war cabinet. Churchill had argued that the plan could not succeed without a large land force. The generals at Gallipoli had requested more men, but Kitchener did not pass on their requests to the War Cabinet.

The Blue Puttees had little time to rest and relax during the wait in Egypt before heading for France and their most deadly battles in the offensive known as the Battle of the Somme. Private W. Tobin said of their stay in Egypt:

> Colonel Hadow[24] was determined to keep us busy. We marched across the dessert. The sun was hot, and men started dropping out. Any man who did not answer the Roll Call after the march was punished. The punishment was *Field Punishment Number 1*. The man was to be tied to a service wagon wheel, but, as we had no wagons, he was tied to a stake for two hours. It got hot in the sun, so the Newfoundlanders would pull the stake out of the sand and go into the shade.[25]

Regardless of this, Hadow held the Newfoundlanders in high regard. He said on January 1916, "My men have done splendidly

---

[24] Lt. Colonel Arthur Hadow of the Newfoundland Regiment.
[25] Ibid.

and I am awfully pleased with them. I only wish I had more. We are reduced to four hundred men."

The Regiment departed from Egypt on March 14, 1916, for Marseilles, France, arriving there on March 20th. From there they went by train to Pont Remy and then marched to Louvencourt. This became their base leading up to the July 1st drive.

Complaints from the Front

Near the end of 1915, letters from some Newfoundland soldiers began appearing in the Newfoundland newspapers, complaining about the conditions they experienced in Europe, . The writers complained that they were sometimes short of food, lacked adequate clothing, didn't get their parcels from home, didn't get their pay on time and some said they were being passed over for promotion because of religious prejudice.

These claims alarmed the Newfoundland Patriotic Association which was making every effort possible to support the troops and to make sure they got all they needed. The Association responded by setting up an investigation into the issue. A key part of the PAN's probe was to question those soldiers who had returned from Europe for various reasons. These included both commissioned and non-commissioned officers.

A witness at the hearing, Lieutenant Gerald Harvey, told the investigation:

> I don't have much sympathy with the newspaper complaints made toward the end of the year. (1915). My reason is that I know a great many of these reports came from people I should not regard seriously. Having been connected with our regiment from the outset, I am aware that there are a certain number of men extremely fond of writing and making things as much public as possible. These men do not express the opinions of their company, even their platoon, and the general opinion among the Battalion will endorse this statement.[26]

While other witnesses, including several privates, agreed with Harvey's sentiments, there had been occasional circumstances

---

[26] PANL MG 632, <u>Minutes of meetings of Newfoundland Patriotic Association</u>.

when the men faced difficulties but with good reason. For a few days in Scotland, their food supplies had been short due to late arrival of supplies. Parcels from home were sometimes late arriving due to problems in transportation to the battlefield. No evidence was found to support the accusation of religious prejudice against members of the Regiment.

Behind the Dardanelles Strategy

It was Winston Churchill's strategy to attack Turkey at a time when the Allies were in a stalemate in France against Germany. He saw this as a means of breaking that stalemate by forcing through the Dardanelles. Had it succeeded, it would have pushed Turkey out of the war and united the Allied forces with their Russian ally.

The plan was supported by Sir Herbert Kitchener and approved by the war cabinet which included Churchill. However, when the campaign collapsed, the Prime Minister and cabinet allowed Churchill to take full blame for the failure, and he was forced to resign from cabinet. Churchill, aided by General Ian Hamilton, who, as Commanding Officer in Gallipoli, was also discredited, persisted with the Prime Minister until he approved access to the minutes of cabinet regarding the Dardanelles' offence.

On the very day that the two found the information that would exonerate them, Kitchener was drowned when the H.M.S. *Hampshire*, on which he was a passenger, struck a German mine and sank. Under these circumstances, rather than cast a shadow on Kitchener's character as one of England's great naval heroes, the Prime Minister refused to release Churchill's findings. Churchill was invited back into cabinet in 1917, but for decades afterwards felt the shame of the failure at the Dardanelles and Gallipoli.

Eventually, the truth came out. The cabinet meetings revealed that Churchill had insisted that the plan could only work if enough land soldiers were involved along with the naval campaign. He stressed that it was essential that whatever land troops were needed must be sent to Gallipoli. The documents also contained twenty-four requests for the 'extra troops' from General Hamilton and Kitchener had kept all twenty-four from cabinet scrutiny.

In later years, another British Prime Minister, Clement Atlee, said of the strategy, "In the whole of the First World War, there was

The graveyard at Gallipoli where many members of the Royal Newfoundland Regiment killed in WWI are buried. (Courtesy Owen and Jean (Carew) Moore)

only one brilliant strategical idea– and that was Winston Churchill's: the Dardanelles."[27]

Yet, it was the worst conducted campaign of WWI with two hundred and fourteen thousand casualties being suffered by the British.[28]

Trade Him to the Turks

The war was not expected to last much longer than four months. Volunteers signed up for one year, but when the war was showing no signs of ending a year later, almost all the Regiment and Naval Reservists decided to stay on and fight. The majority of those who did not re-enlist had legitimate reasons for getting out. Usually, their reason was they were desperately needed at home to support a family, or because of sickness or wounds received in battle. However, three Regiment privates raised the ire of Governor Davidson when they refused to re-enlist without valid reasons. When told of the three, he advised the Newfoundland

---

[27] William Manchester, The Last Lion.
[28] The Twentieth Century an Almanac.

Regiment's Adjutant at Headquarters that, "On no account, is he to accept any of these 'fair weather' soldiers for re-enlistment."

One of the three, a Lebanese immigrant to Newfoundland, who trained with the Newfoundland Regiment in Scotland, drew sarcastic criticism from the Governor. He said:

> Morgannam is a Syrian from Lebanon and may be technically a Turkish subject. If arrangements are being made for an exchange of British and Turkish civilians, he might prove of some little use if he were sent for exchange to the Turkish authorities, so as to release a British subject. I do not think that with his present record, he would be a source of danger to the British forces if on arrival in Turkey, he were compelled to join the Turkish troops.[29]

Davidson sought to help returning veterans whenever possible. Vincent Walsh, who was wounded in Gallipoli and honourably discharged from the Regiment in 1915, was given a term of employment at Government House by Governor Davidson. After a period of rest and some health care, Walsh passed a medical and was welcomed back into the Newfoundland Constabulary which he had left to go overseas. On July 20, 1917, Governor Davidson, after consulting with Inspector General of Police John Sullivan, hired Walsh to serve a term as orderly at Government House. Sullivan told the Governor, "I look upon him as being thoroughly trustworthy and will be glad to transfer him from the Constabulary force to your Excellency's service." When Davidson's term as Governor ended, Walsh was transferred back to the constabulary.

---

[29] PANL GN 1/3/A Box 97.

Chapter 5

DOOMED OFFENCES

Not Ready for July 1st

Although the generals were confident of their decision to launch the Somme offensive on July 1, 1916, there were warnings that the Germans were better prepared than the Allies and that the offensive should be delayed. One of these warnings came from George Phillips, a young Newfoundland private, who had spent a night behind enemy lines at Beaumont Hamel and pleaded with senior officers for a delay. Another warning came from Winston Churchill, a then young member of the war-cabinet, who had made frequent visits to the front, recommended to parliament that they intervene to delay the offensive. The Somme was a long river in France, and what was expected to be a single battle became a long and drawn out series of battles starting at Beaumont Hamel.

The private who warned his officers was killed two months later, but a comrade in battle, Walter Day, lived to tell Phillip's story. Day is said to have been the youngest person to have signed up for the Newfoundland Regiment in WWI. He was tall and, through hard work in helping his family at home, was in good physical shape. Although fourteen, he had the appearances of an eighteen or nineteen year old. Walter marked his fifteenth birthday as a member of the Regiment. By the time he fought at Beaumont Hamel on July 1st, he was already an experienced soldier. He was among the fortunate ones who survived the Battle of Beaumont Hamel and the war.

Almost sixty years later, Walter Day could still recall with great detail the Great War and its hardships, battles and disasters. The story of Private George Phillips was embedded in his memory. He described Phillips as a courageous soldier and "...a real man in battle." Several days before Beaumont Hamel, Phillips was part of a patrol that while scouting no-man's-land at night, engaged in a battle with the enemy that left several Newfoundland soldiers dead. Phillips survived and made it back to his Battalion the next morning demanding to talk with his commanding officers.

Phillips described the battle and explained that he spent the night in a German trench. He brought back buttons and a badge from a German tunic to verify how far he had gotten. When he came face to face with his commanding officer, he said, "Never make that drive because every German over there has a machine gun waiting for us."[1]

George Phillips was awarded the Military Medal and the Russian Cross.[2] He was killed in battle at Gueudecourt, France, on October 12, 1916.

Churchill Wanted a Delay on July 1st

Winston Churchill advised parliament that the Germans were better prepared than the Generals believed and that the Somme offensive should be delayed to allow time to improve Allied strength and readiness. After visiting the trenches, Churchill put forward a series of suggestions to improve things for the fighting men and to make them at least as comfortable and protected as were the German troops.

To improve troop logistics, he recommended that the British construct a network of light railways behind the lines. He pointed out that the German trenches were better constructed and their trench lighting was superior to the British. Churchill said that an immediate improvement in the lighting should be a priority. Another problem that he felt could be remedied immediately was the shortage of steel helmets in the trenches. He concluded his parliamentary remarks with a recommendation that the troops at the front be rotated to spread the burden of suffering and risk.

After Lloyd George asked him to be his 'eyes and ears' on the battlefront, Churchill, himself a pilot, flew over to France every morning in his own plane to observe conditions at the front. He walked away from several crashes and near accidents and on one occasion, although cut and bleeding, went directly to Parliament to deliver a speech before seeking medical attention. When all was said and done, the authorities ignored all of these suggestions. The resulting doomed offensives troubled Churchill more than any other aspect of the government's war policy.

Winston Churchill repeatedly criticized the military strategists for their handling of the war. His criticism was accompanied by positive suggestions which sometimes were accepted. For example, his recommendation to use convoys to combat the threat of German

---

[1] Joy Cave, <u>What Became of Corporal Pittman?</u>
[2] G.W. Nicholson, <u>The Fighting Newfoundlander</u>.

U-boats was adopted in 1917 and resulted in a reduction in the loss of merchant ship tonnage from 874,576 to 351,105 [3]

The young Churchill, already a veteran of war, raised eyebrows among the British establishment when he criticized the war effort saying that staff officers, safely out of range of enemy gunfire, were outrageously pinning medals on each other. He was firm in the belief that Parliament's sympathy should be focussed on the non-commissioned officers and the regimental officers. He said, "Honour should go where death and danger goes."[4]

Canadian military historians, Desmond Morton and J.L. Granatstein in their book *Marching to Armageddon*, commenting on the Somme, said:

> Haig and historians would argue about its value. The few who knew what the Somme had cost Britain in the quality of its young men as much as in the appalling numbers felt numb and then furious with frustration. Yet Haig had insisted that the war could not be won until the German army was defeated and was there another way?

The Famous 29th

The first of many offensives that comprised the Battle of the Somme was the attack on the impregnable village of Beaumont Hamel, France, on July 1, 1916. Leading the way in this assault was the famous 29th Division of the 8th Army which included the Newfoundland Regiment under the command of Lieutenant-General Sir Aylmer Hunter-Weston, nicknamed by the ranks "Hunter-Bunter." During WWII there was a hostel on Water Street West called the Red Triangle, similar to the Knights of Columbus on Military Road, both of which were built and operated to serve the soldiers visiting or stationed in the city. The name "Red Triangle," representing a half diamond, was a revered and inspirational name among Newfoundlanders for decades because it was the emblem for the 29th Division in WWI.

This historic emblem was designed by Major-General Sir Beauvoir de Lisle, divisional commander of the 29th Division, to

---

[3] William Manchester, <u>The Last Lion</u>.
[4] Ibid.

remind all ranks of the value of the diamond as a military formation in open fighting from a patrol to an army.[5]

> *Oh, this is the song of the Twenty-ninth,*
> *On every field you'll find it.*
> *For wherever the Red Triangle went*
> *It left its mark behind it*
> — The Song of the 29th Division by
> Lancelot Cayley Shadwell

Battalions not Regiments

There was a difference in how wars were fought in WWI and WWII. In WWI, the British fought by battalions rather than regiments. In order to follow the trail of the Red Triangle on the July 1st drive, it is necessary to understand the British Army structure in that war. The British 8th Army Corps which included Newfoundlanders was made up of three divisions. These were the 29th Division, 31st Division and the 4th Division. A Division was made up of three Brigades, with each Brigade having four Battalions. The three Brigades making up the 29th were the 86th, 87th, and 88th Brigades. The Newfoundland Battalion was a part of the 88th Brigade.

The three infantry Brigades were supported by artillery—normally seventy-six guns. Of these, fifty-four were eighteen-pounders, eighteen were 4.5 howitzers and four were sixty-pounders. There were twenty-four machine guns to each division.

A battalion consisted of 992 other ranks and thirty officers. The Battalion was sub-divided into four companies and each company consisted of four platoons, and there were four sections to each Platoon.

The four Battalions that comprised the 88th Brigade included: the 1st Battalion of the Newfoundland Regiment, the 4th Worcestershire Regiment, 2nd Hampshire Regiment, and the 1st Essex Regiment.[6]

---

[5] B. Joy Cave, <u>Whatever Became of Corporal Pittman</u>.
[6] G.W.L. Nicholson, <u>The Fighting Newfoundlander, A History of The Royal Newfoundland Regiment</u>.

The Second Contingent of Newfoundland Regiment Volunteers leaving on the *Florizel*. Due to hat shortage they were outfitted with balaclava hats. Their arrival in Scotland caused rumours that the Russians had landed there. (PANL)

Germans had Advantage

Although the Germans did not know the starting date of the Allied offensive, they fully anticipated it. In fact, they applied their time effectively in strengthening their defences. The natural geographic layout of the surrounding area had already given them advantages. In 1915, the Germans built up the defences of Beaumont-Hamel. A formidable complex of trenches was dug and constructively reinforced with an endless barbed-wire fence. They dug deeply in order to assure that they remained dry, comfortable and almost artillery proof.

Private homes in the village of Beaumont Hamel were converted into fortresses where they stored ammunition and stationed snipers. Small concrete forts were built at crucial points. One was located on Redan Ridge and another on Hawthorn Ridge overlooking no-man's-land. Both ran south-easterly and Beaumont Hamel lay halfway up a gully running between them.

The northern boundary of the target lay at four miles south of a place called Gommecourt. Not far from this, travelling northeast, was Serre another heavily fortified village. This area played a crucial role in the disastrous events unfolding that day.

Directly in front of the British trenches was an incline that led across the battlefield and rose in the east beneath ridge after ridge occupied by the enemy. German trenches on each side of the road controlled access by that route between Beaumont Hamel and Serre. Adding to the strong German fortifications were two more obstacles to overcome. There was Hawthorne Mine, an old chalk mine near the Redan Ridge which the enemy had converted into a very strong defensive position. Then there was "Y" Ravine, a steep sided cliff, just behind the German front line trenches. The Germans had concealed many machine guns there which later helped decimate the Newfoundland Regiment.

Agonizing Training

In preparation for the July 1st Drive, the Newfoundland Regiment went through daily rigorous training. Despite the regularity of cool and wet weather, the men remained committed and energetic throughout.

The officer in charge of this phase of activity was Brigadier-General D.E. Cayley who would order the Newfoundlanders to repeat an exercise two and three times before he was satisfied with their progress. This was no ordinary fifteen or sixty minute drill. Historian G. W. Nicholson described the training and the men who were subjected to it. He said:

> The demands that these exercises made on the men were such as only troops in first-class physical condition - as the Newfoundlanders were - could have met. To carry out the attack once meant covering a good ten miles between leaving billets and getting back to them, and everything had to be done in full fighting order, sometimes at the double, sometimes charging with the bayonet, sometimes digging, but always on the move.[7]

As if that were not enough, the afternoons were occupied with drill on trench clearing. For this the men were marched to and from the demonstration field. This was followed by other training that would be ordered by the commanding officer. Remarkably,

---

[7] G.W.L. Nicholson, The Fighting Newfoundlander,A History of The Royal Newfoundland Regiment, p249.

following a physically exhaustive day of training, it would take just one soldier to sing or hum, "Keep the Home Fires Burning", or "A Long Way to Tipperary" and the others would perk up and join in. Little wonder their spirit and discipline were so widely praised.

Patrols Go Behind German Line

The Newfoundland Regiment occupied positions in the front line trenches opposite Beaumont Hamel during April, May and June. Their first fatality in France was Private G. Curnew who was killed by a sniper on April 24, 1916. An important task for Newfoundlanders during this period was to send patrols into no-man's-land to gather intelligence about the German defences. They confirmed what Winston Churchill had been telling General Haig that the enemy defences were well prepared and their soldiers vigilant.[8]

The Germans captured one of these patrols. Among those captured was Private Thomas Coombs who wrote home on July 18, 1916:

> I was captured June 28th at 1 a.m. with five other fellows, one dead, two wounded and one unwounded with me. It was quite an exciting time and I consider myself lucky not to have got bowled over, not that I relish the idea of being in my present condition, but one must put up with the fortunes of war.[9]

The Germans were not the only enemy our troops had to face in France. When the Newfoundland Battalion began occupying the trenches in April 1916, they encountered for the first time the "Somme Rat." Military historian Nicholson described it as, "...a breed unsurpassed in size and daring anywhere along the Front. Some said they were bigger than cats."

The soldiers in the trenches were forced to take extra precautions to protect their rations. Simply storing unused rations in one's haversack was no answer to the problem because this large rat would destroy the haversack to get to the food. Many times the gunfire heard at night was from soldiers firing at rats roaming the trenches throughout the night.

---

[8] John Pearson, <u>The Private Lives of Winston Churchill</u>.
[9] Dr. David Facey-Crowther, <u>Better Than the Best, The Royal Newfoundland Regiment</u>.

The Regimental cooking equipment was brought up to the front lines at Beaumont Hamel so the troops could have a hot meal on the day of the Battle of Beaumont Hamel. This was the first of a series of battles in the overall battle known as "The Battle of the Somme." (IWM)

The Eve of the July 1st Drive

The Newfoundland Regiment arrived in the village of Louvencourt, France, on June 30, 1916, a beautiful summer's day. 776 non-commissioned-officers and men, and twenty-five officers and their commanding officers answered the 9:00 p.m. roll call. After this, they began moving to their battle positions. About 200 yards down the road, a soldier bravely broke into singing "Keep the Home Fires Burning", and the entire regiment joined in. The spontaneity of the Regimental sing-a-long bolstered its spirit but it was not an easy march. The Germans had recently shelled the road which forced the soldiers to cross the open fields in single file.

While the Newfoundlanders marched, British field guns hammered away at the German trenches, and the men settled down for the night 300 yards from the enemy. Their optimistic mood was generated by their training and knowledge that heavy artillery was already pounding the enemy trenches. They were confident of achieving their objective.

The British trenches along the way were given familiar names like Tipperary Avenue which was the communication trench south of Auchonvillers. Other trench names reflected the hometowns and streets of Newfoundland. The Newfoundlanders had to remain at Tipperary Avenue until their fellow battalions caught up with them. The names were placed on maps as a means of identifying troops and their movements.

By 2:30 a.m., they had moved another 750 yards to the St. John's Road trenches directly opposite the Y Ravine, behind the German front line trenches. By that time they had been marching for five hours. Although tired, most were too anxious to sleep. Here they took on more supplies, including trench bridges and Bangalore torpedoes which they needed for the next day's battle. A Bangalore torpedo was a metal pipe filled with explosives used to detonate land mines or to clear a path through barbed wire. At dawn on July 1st, they were fed hot food which was delivered from the regimental cooks assembled in the nearby woods.[10]

Anxiety was widespread among the men throughout the night prior to the offensive. They smoked tobacco and chatted with each other and struggled to find comfort in the cold, damp, and inhospitable foxhole. Officers spent their time carrying out last minute inspections and preparations. At 6:25 a.m. an intensive bombardment began. At 7:20 a.m. the officers met with the brigade major to synchronise watches.

A Mule's Burden

The life of an infantryman at the front was not easy. Muddy trenches and battlefields, gnawing hunger, enemy bombardment and the constant noise of artillery shelling were not their only challenges. When the infantryman moved into battle, he was burdened with a minimum of sixty-six pounds of equipment to carry with him. Each soldier carried a backpack containing shaving gear and extra socks, the unconsumed portion of the day's ration allowance, special emergency rations, a gas helmet and goggles, field dressings and iodine. In addition, he carried a rolled ground sheet, a water bottle, a steel helmet, an entrenching tool, wire cutters, a mess-tin, two sandbags, 220 rounds of ammunition and a rifle. Besides their basic load, most carried shovels, picks, wire, corkscrew stakes, extra bombs, flares and other items.[11]

---

[10] Ibid.
[11] B. Joy Cave, <u>What Became of Corporal Pittman</u>.

When new steel helmets were passed out to members of the Newfoundland Regiment in France during the summer of 1916, British senior officers were upset by a novel use Newfoundlanders found for them.

A common reaction from the soldiers was the comment, "If they are not proof against bullets, they are a proof against shrapnel." Yet, this did not dampen the troops enthusiasm towards the helmet when they discovered an alternate use for them. They found that the helmets made convenient cooking pots on the front. One soldier said, "They are beyond all praise. There is nothing you cannot cook in them: eggs, tea, soup, are all excellent."

Senior officers were not impressed and warned that severe penalties would be handed out if the practice continued. In response, the soldiers found a new use for the helmet– a wash pan to bath with. There were no further threats from the officers because far more important issues had to be dealt with in the days leading up to the start of the Battle of the Somme.[12]

The Problems of the Red Triangle

To achieve its goal at Beaumont Hamel, the 29th Division was assigned the formidable task of breaking through the Germans left flank. This meant pushing the Germans northward towards the heavily fortified village of Serre. The task was gruelling because they had to accomplish this mission without capturing the German batteries at Redan and Hawthorn Ridges.

Before proceeding with their attack plan, senior officers carefully analyzed four options:

(1) The first plan considered was a frontal attack on Serre. This was impractical because not only would it have been necessary to take out the Redan and Hawthorn batteries, but they would also have to take Beaumont Hamel. A mission of this sort would have taken too long a time.

(2) The second option involved attacking along the northern ridge and coming up on the rear of Beaumont Hamel to isolate it. The weakness in this was that it would expose the British to an attack from the village of Serre.

---

[12] The Evening Telegram, July 1916.

(3) The third option which required a right hand attack over the southern ridge at Hawthorn would expose the battalion on the slopes connecting it with Serre.

(4) The fourth option was less inviting than the other three. It involved moving troops down the valley between Redan and Hawthorn Ridges from a place called Auchonvillers. Such an attack would make the men easy targets for every German heavy artillery gun within range.

The only practical course of action was to come up with a compromise battle plan. Yet, even the compromise plan adopted was perilous. Their final decision was to mount two main attacks at the same time over both the northern and southern ridges. The 31st Division was assigned to protect the left flank of the assault troops battling for Redan Ridge. From there, the 31st were to turn northeast and drive the Germans from their stronghold at Serre. In the centre, another force would advance down the ridge to link with the attacking forces to the north and south. The adopted plan was integrated into the overall strategy used in the offensive.

Battle of the Somme

The Somme Offensive began at Beaumont Hamel on July 1, 1916, along a sixteen mile front with the Newfoundland Regiment, and the 29th Division, playing a key role.

The offensive started at 7:20 a.m. when the mine at Hawthorne Ridge, overlooking no-man's-land, was blown up. According to regimental history one soldier said, "The Germans first sight after taking up their positions was of wave after wave of British troops crawling out of their trenches, and coming towards them at a walk, with their bayonets glistening in the sun." The Battle of Beaumont Hamel had started.

When the troops of the 29th Division left their own trenches, their only covering fire was a thin barrage of eighteen-pounder guns, Stokes mortars, and machine guns.

At 7:30 a.m. the Inniskilling Fusiliers, South Wales Borderers and the Royal Fusiliers and Lancaster Fusiliers, all Battalions with the 29th Division, attacked. They were to clear the way for the Newfoundland Regiment to carry out a frontal attack on the stronghold at Beaumont Hamel, but were nearly wiped out in the battle. The same fate greeted the next wave of attack that included: the Kings Own Scottish Borderers, Border Regiment, Middlesex Regiment and Dublin Fusiliers.

The Timing was Contentious

The great Hawthorn Mine was blown up on schedule. Forty thousand pounds of ammonal gas hidden sixty-five feet below the German strong-point named Hawthorn Redoubt was detonated. A thousand yards away, Newfoundlanders waiting to go into battle felt the minor earthquake and saw the gigantic clouds of smoke, earth, stones and debris climbing hundreds of feet into the air.

During the strategic meetings prior to the attack, the timing of the mine explosion was a contentious issue. General Hunter Weston and General Douglas Haig were at odds over the timing to blow up the Mine. Weston favoured doing it at 3:30 a.m., in darkness, four hours before the major offensive started. He argued that this action would enable the British to move in and occupy the crater before the offensive began at 7:30 a.m. Weston was convinced that the timing of such an explosion would create a false sense of security among the enemy because it would be followed by a four hour lull leading up to the start of the offensive and thereby causing confusion.

Haig disagreed. He was convinced that such a strategy could backfire and the Germans, with a proven efficiency in being able to quickly move in and occupy such mine craters, would turn the situation to their favour. Following much debate, the generals made a compromise to blow up the mine ten minutes before the 7:30 a.m. deadline.

Unfortunately, this removed the element of surprise from the attack and turned out to be another contributing factor to the tragedy of that day. As a preliminary to the 7:30 a.m. offensive, the artillery launched a bombardment on the German front line at 6:25 a.m. This had to be interrupted at 7:20 a.m. to allow the British time to move in and take control of the crater. At this crucial time, the offensive lost the important diversion they needed.

Due to confusion of the all clear signal to be given by the first two waves of attackers, the commanding officers at headquarters ordered the Newfoundland Regiment[13] into battle at 8:40 a.m. then

---

[13] Although, the Newfoundland Regiment became a Battalion, the references to Newfoundland Regiment continued to be used when describing the Newfoundland Battalion.

countermanded the order. At 9:15 a.m. the order was repeated, and this time the Regiment moved immediately across no-man's-land. A hundred yards ahead of them the front line was covered with the dead and wounded from the previous attacks.

"Deadmen can advance no farther."

A strategic plan devised to protect soldiers during battle backfired and contributed to the casualties during the July 1st Drive. Each soldier had been required to sew on a triangular piece of tin 18 cm. (7 in.) on each side on the back of his uniform between the shoulders to identify Allied soldiers for the aircraft providing air cover during battle. However, the sun reflecting off the metal pinpointed wounded soldiers attempting to return to their lines, and made them easy targets for enemy snipers.[14]

The Germans, having wiped out the first two waves of attacks, now concentrated all their guns on the advancing Newfoundlanders. Thirty minutes later it was all over. Most of the Newfoundlanders were gunned down near the "Danger Tree", which was at a gap in the British barbed wire. Private Jim Steel recalled what happened:

We were all knocked out before reaching the German trenches. I was knocked over myself about twenty yards from their trenches, with shrapnel which struck me in the head after breaking through my steel helmet. I managed to crawl back to our own trenches, 450 yards at 11:00 p.m.[15]

According to author Joseph R. Smallwood:

When Lt. Colonel Hadow (Newfoundland Battalion) reported the failure of the attack to Brigadier-General Cayley[16] at Brigade Battle Headquarters, despite his expressing shock at the extent of the casualties, Cayley ordered Hadow to regroup the men and make a fresh assault. Cooler heads prevailed and the order was later rescinded.

[14] R. Joseph Smallwood, editor-in-chief, Encyclopedia of Newfoundland and Labrador, Newfoundland Publishers (1967) Limited.
[15] Dr. David Facey-Crowther, Better Than the Best the Royal Newfoundland Regiment.
[16] Nicholson's book, The Fighting Newfoundlander lists Cayley's rank at Beaumont Hamel as Major General D. E. Cayley.

The next day, only sixty-eight out of a force of 801 officers and men answered roll call. There were 710 wounded, killed or missing. A few more made it back to camp over the next several days and others were forced to remain in shell holes because of snipers. Some got mixed up with other regiments. Private Ron Dunne, himself hit by enemy fire, recalled:

> I got up out of the trench, the boys were falling on either side until there were only two of us left. He got it, he was killed. Then I got it. I got two bullets in me. I dropped. Blood was coming out of me. I thought they saw me go down. I stopped the blood as best I could. The sun was pouring down and they were shelling, the Germans were. I was there all day and night. Sunday come. I lived through Sunday but when the sun went down, I give up. I said my prayers and I seen my Mom, as far as I knew, but I knew she wasn't there. They picked me up and I don't know who. I don't know how I got to hospital where they operated and took the metal out of me.[17]

The Commanding Officer of the 88th Brigade, Major General D. E. Cayley, said of the performance of the Newfoundland Regiment on that day, "It was a magnificent display of trained and disciplined valour and only failed because dead men can advance no farther."

WWI historian, Captain B. H. Liddell, described the Battle of Beaumont Hamel as, "...an epic of heroism, and, better still, the proof of the moral quality of the new armies of Britain, who, in making their supreme sacrifice of the war, passed through the most fiery and bloody of ordeals with their courage unshaken and their fortitude established.[18]

A Landmark in History

The July 1st Somme Offensive proved to be a landmark in the history of WWI. It was at this point in the war that the British assumed the major role in the western front campaign. Winston Churchill, writing in his essay on Sir Douglas Haig, balanced his criticism of the General by noting:

[17] Ibid.
[18] Captain B.H. Liddell, The Real War 1914-1918.

The first use of a gas attack at the Western Front during WWI. (NAC)

It was not until the Somme in July 1916 that we became a major factor in the vast land conflict. The next two years shows the British war effort, casualties and will-to-conquer as always equal to the French, and ultimately dominant. It was over this period that Haig presided. No one can say that it did not end in victory.[19]

By the time the Battle of the Somme came to an end in November 1916, the total British casualties were 19,240 dead and 38,230 wounded. According to the *Encyclopaedia of Newfoundland and Labrador*:

> No Regiment suffered as many losses as did the Newfoundland Regiment. It was several days before a complete count could be ascertained. Then the report was fourteen officers and 219 other ranks dead, twelve officers and 374 other ranks wounded, ninety-one other ranks missing. Of the officers of the Newfoundland Regiment who went into battle all received wounds or died in action.

---

[19] Winston Churchill, <u>Great Contemporaries</u>, Collins Clear-Type Press, London and Glasgow, 1937.

St. John's Wood

News of the tragedy of the July 1st Drive travelled slowly from across the Atlantic in 1916, and it took weeks for Newfoundlanders to learn the full extent of the tragedy at Beaumont Hamel. However, the French Government moved quickly to honour the courage displayed by the Newfoundland Regiment on July 1st by officially renaming the field of battle where so much Newfoundland blood was shed in defence of the Allied cause.

Within days after the starting offensive in the Battle of the Somme, the battlefield at Beaumont Hamel was officially named 'St. John's Wood.' H. Winter, editor of the *Evening Telegram*, wrote in his column on July 20th, 1916:

> It is a rare compliment, this naming of the field of battle, after our capital implying a rare gallantry that deserved it. Newfoundlanders in London will be reminded in years to come of 'St. John's Wood' by the coincidence that one of that great city's pleasantest districts bears the same name.

Referring to the field, Winter described the many small patches of dark forest, "...that break up the sunny landscape. The battle has since surged far beyond it. Before it sleep quietly some of those we knew. It bears, in their honour, the name of the city which they loved. It is St. John's Wood."

Sadly, the name did not endure, and there is no mention of the honour even in the brochures handed out to today's visitors to Beaumont Hamel.

The Blue Puttees Move on Hawthorn Ridge

The taking of Hawthorn Ridge was assigned to the 29th Division which had the task of bringing up the rear in that encounter. The front to which the 29th had been assigned spread over a distance of 2000 yards. They were given three objectives and the furthest of these, Puisieux Trench, about three miles ahead of their position, was assigned to the Newfoundland Battalion.

The remaining two brigades in the 29th Division, the 86th and 87th were assigned the job of clearing the way for the 88th Newfoundland Battalion. The 86th was given the task of clearing the way up on the left which led to a point in front of Beaumont Hamel. The 87th took the right which was in front of Y Ravine and also led to the point near Beaumont Hamel. When that assignment was completed the two Brigades were to move to their second target which was the German Intermediate Line near Beaumont Hamel Road. Once they had achieved this objective, the Newfoundlanders were to pass through the other two brigades and keep on advancing until they had completed their mission.[20]

Fatal Error

The success of the Newfoundland Regiment's task depended on a pre-determined signal devised by the military strategists. Once the 87th Brigade achieved its first objective and cleared the way for the Newfoundlanders, they were to fire a white flare. Upon this signal being given, the Newfoundland Regiment was to begin its attack on the German stronghold.

An unanticipated coincidence with deadly consequences occurred at the start of the battle. When General Beauvoir de Lisle was told that the white flares had been fired by the 87th Brigade, he gave orders for the 88th Brigade to attack the enemy's front line but to keep two battalions back as divisional reserves. What the General did not know that day was that white flares were also being used by the Germans to signal to their artillery that their guns were not on target.

Another setback was that the Germans were not as unprepared as Haig had expected. German observers had witnessed major artillery movements, lanes being cut through the British barbed-wire, and the bridging of the rear trenches. Author Joy Cave provided insight into the extent of the German's awareness of the pending offensive. She said:

> The German army of that time was one of the finest professional fighting machines the world has ever seen: it would have been difficult to hoodwink, even supposing anyone had tried to do so. In the event no one tried. The element of surprise, tactically so important in the battle was completely absent from the preparations for the Somme.[21]

---

[20] Forgotten Heroes, a publication of the Royal Newfoundland Regiment, 1981.
[21] This problem was overcome at Cambrai where General Tudor's strategies were applied.

The British might just as well have printed large posters saying 'Very soon now we are going to mount an attack.'

In Sheffield on June 1st, the Parliamentary Secretary to the Ministry of Munitions had appealed for a postponement of the Bank Holiday. On June 2nd, Labour Advisor to Government, Arthur Henderson told munition workers, 'It should suffice that we ask for a postponement to the end of July. This fact should speak volumes.' It did.[22]

Newspaper reports of the speech made their way into the hands of Crown Prince Rupprecht of Bavaria, a German Army commander who shared the information with other military leaders. This information, added to the intelligence already gathered, convinced the Germans that a major offensive was being planned. Not knowing the specific date, they shrewdly drilled their front line troops on how to respond when the assault started.

When the Hawthorne Mine blew up, the front line German Reserve Regiment recognized that the beginning of the major offensive had started, and they promptly responded as they had been trained to do. The Germans guarding the mine were killed in the explosion, but the remaining German soldiers got ready on the lower steps of their dugouts, rifles in hand, waiting for the barrage to lift. Before the smoke cleared, they were moving in to occupy the craters as Haig had feared.

In the *Times of London's History of World War I*, the claim is made that the Newfoundland soldier who advanced farthest at Beaumont Hamel on July 1, 1916 was Company Sergeant Major W. Clare. This claim has been made by a succession of writers over the past 100 years, all basing their stories on the *London Time's* history. Colonel G.W Nicholson, historian, countered this claim by pointing out that the British military received the statement of an officer, not named, who provided an eye witness account. The officer stated:

> Clair did get quite a distance, but he was taking cover in the vicinity where I was lying. On that morning (July 1st) Ralph Herder, Lance Corporal Ralph Andrews and Private Jack Caul got as near to the German Front line as any survivor of that awful day.[23]

---

[22] B. Joy Cave, <u>What Became of Corporal Pittman</u>.
[23] PANL MG 439 Box 1.

Word of the military disaster at Beaumont Hamel reached Newfoundland in bits and pieces for weeks after the July 1st battle. There were few dry eyes anywhere in the colony when the battle accounts like the following began appearing in local newspapers. Two weeks after the battle, the *Evening Telegram* told the story.

The newspaper heading read: "Newfoundlanders Charge Hopeless Task. Survivors' Accounts–Wounded Shot on Rescuer's Back. "Newfoundlanders I salute you individually. You have done better than the best."

"Thus said the General to the men of the Newfoundland Regiment after its great attack on July 1st".*(Daily Mail,* July 1914)

The article read:

The Newfoundlanders were given what is now recognized to have been an impossible task, and ,although they failed, the story of their bravery and daring will live forever. The regiment had been in reserve waiting to take its appointed place in the great attack– the capture of the third line of German trenches immediately in front of them. The task of capturing the first and second lines was assigned to English line regiments.

'All the German lines,' says the eyewitness, 'were raked with hundreds of thousands of shells. It seemed impossible that anything could still be alive. Suddenly the artillery lifted and the English regiments attacked. As if, by magic the German lines swarmed with men, and machine guns belched out from behind ruins, and from the mouth of hidden pits, and even from shell holes. The British troops did not waver, but they melted away, and not many reached the German lines. More shells screamed across this land of dead men, and then other troops rushed to the attack. Again the German machine guns took their toll, and again the attack failed.

'Now came the turn of the Newfoundlanders. The fate which had overtaken their comrades daunted them not one bit. These boys, their average age was under twenty-four, were as steady as veterans, as steady as on that parade at St. John's when they embarked for England to fight for the

Empire. Not a man hesitated. With a cheer, they were over the parapet and with the Colonel, *Fighting Chitral Haddo* in the van, attempted the impossible.

Officers fell right and left, but as they fell they waved their men on. "Right to it this time,' was the cry. A second lieutenant speedily found himself in charge of a company, and as he fell, a sergeant sprang forward to take his place. Companies melted away, but as each man fell he always cried, 'Now right on boys, right to it this time!' That was their slogan, and bounding from shell-hole to shell-hole these gallant lads struggled towards the German lines. A few reached the German wire, which marvelous to relate, was almost intact, but they could do no mare. The charge was over– they had failed, but in brave company, for at the outset they all realized that what had been impossible for eight English regiments was not possible for them.

There are now, just behind the British lines in this quarter of the field, a few mounds of earth which no Newfoundlander fails to salute–the burial ground of those who fell on July 1. Reserves volunteered to a man to recover their dead, and under a galling fire from German rifles and guns they performed their task. 'We wanted those at home,' said one who did his share, 'to know that our comrades sleep easily; that the padre has said the prayer for the dead and that we who live, to bring the Germans to account.'

Letters Home Tell of July 1st on Battlefield

A letter written by a Newfoundland soldier, less than a week after the famous Battle of Beaumont Hamel, presented one of the most moving first-hand-accounts of the heroism of Newfoundlanders on July 1, 1916. The letter, written by Bert Ellis to his mother, Mrs. J. E. Ellis, 60 Springdale Street, St. John's, Newfoundland, was published in the *Evening Telegram* on July 22, 1916, under the heading "The Story of Their Heroism– A sight never to be forgotten." It read:

My Dear Mother,
How glad I am to be able to write to you once again even though I have it to do on my back. I have a lot to be

thankful for. No doubt you have heard all about our big drive by this time, or you will by the time you get this. I will try and tell you as briefly as possibly how it happened. The Newfoundland Regiment in France is about done. They stood to their guns almost to the last man, and fought like those who knew no fear. When the roll was called only forty-three answered it, and out of that number two were from C Company. Certainly that's not counting the wounded, but I can't say how many were killed or wounded. I think there were more wounded than killed.

We got out of our trenches on Saturday (July 1st) morning, about 9:30. It was a lovely morning, and one never to be forgotten by British soldiers. The 29th Division had one of the worst parts of the line to take, and they took it, but what a price they paid, what a sacrifice of our bravest and our best. It unnerves me to think of it. In the Division are three brigades, the 86th, 87th, and 88th. The last one was attached to altogether between 16,000 and 20,000 men. The 86th had to take the first line, the 87th the second, and we had to take the third line of trenches. Well, our men fell so fast that we had to go up and reinforce the 86th Brigade. The first Brigade had nothing to compare with like what we had.

It was like Hell let loose. The smoke of guns and noise of shells bursting was something never to be forgotten, not to speak of the machine gun fire, which mowed our men down like wheat before the scythe. No doubt you know what a noise the 'air hammer' makes at the dock when they are working; well, that's something like a machine gun sounds when in action. They played havoc with our men, and to make matters worse, they had practically on both sides, what is called enfilading fire[24], which is the worst kind of fire to be under. You could almost see the bullets coming, they came so thick and fast. I got over between the first and second lines before I got hit. I got it in the right leg about four inches from the ankle, and strange to say, the first one was a bullet, then a piece of shell struck me in the same place.

---

[24]A volley of gun fire along a line, end to end is called enfilading fire.

When I was crawling back, that's what puzzles me most – however I got back, I was all alone, and never met a soul all the way back, which was about four hundred yards, only dead! dead! everywhere!

The awful sight, it made me so sick that I used to lie down, and wonder if I would go on or stay there. It wouldn't have been so bad only they turned the guns on us as we were trying to get back. Our boys acted throughout like heroes. They went up on top singing just as if they were going on a march, instead of facing death. The place we went over, or just in front of us was called - the 'Happy Valley' or 'The Vale of Death'.

It put me in mind of Buckmaster's Field, with the German trenches on LeMarchant Road, and ours up by 'Adams', so when we came on the sky line they just mowed us down, but our boys showed no fear.[25]

It will be some time before I can walk, but my leg is not broken for which I can thank God. Tom Kelly's brother Ern, is in the same ward with me, so you can tell Tom he is wounded, in the right arm, so it will be a bit difficult for him to write for some time.

The shrapnel bullet went right through his arm, just above his wrist. Tell the family the same address as mine will do for him, and will find him all right. Well, dear, I think this must do for the present as I find it a bit tiresome on my back. Everything possible is done for us here, so don't worry about me. Cheer up, and don't be downhearted. Love to all the friends at home, we will have victory soon.

Yours with love,
– Bert

Private Jim McGrath's Letter Home

On July 31, 1916, the following letter written by Private James McGrath of St. John's, Newfoundland, and sent to his mother was

---

[25] Buckmaster's Field is now Buckmasters Circle. Adams, refers to the residence of former Mayor William Adams at the corner of Adams Avenue and Pennywell Road.

published in *The Evening Telegram*. Young McGrath was wounded in the July 1st offensive. It was written from his hospital bed in the 3rd London General Hospital on July 7, 1916.

Dear Mother,
It gives me great pleasure in taking up my pencil to write you a line; by the time you get this you'll know all about the Regiment, they got a terrible cutting up. I suppose you have already seen by the casualty list where I was wounded but not serious. I am wounded in both legs, right arm and a little below the hip.

I will tell you the 1st of July 1916, I will never forget. We advanced on the German trenches at 10 in the morning and the machine gun fire was something terrible; well they actually mowed us down like sheep; anyway, I managed to get to their barbed wire where I got the first shot, then went to jump into their trench when I got the second in the leg. I lay in no-man's land for 15 hours, and when I went to crawl, which is a distance of a mile and a quarter, they fired on me again. This time fetching me in the left leg, and so I waited for another hour and moved again, only having the use of my left arm now.

As I was doing splendidly, nearing our own trench, they again fetched me, this time around the hip as I crawled on. I managed to get to our own line which I saw was evacuated as our artillery was playing heavy on their trenches, they retaliated which kept me in a hole for another hour anyway. I was then rescued by Captain Windeler who took me on his back to the dressing station a distance of two miles.

Well, thank God, my wounds are all flesh wounds and won't take long to heal up. As far as I can hear, there was only one hundred answered roll call and Jim Saunders is one of them. I am glad to hear Jim is well. The hospital I am now in is the 3rd London General Hospital, a swell place with lots of food and nourishment. I haven't much more news to tell you at present; you must excuse this writing for this is the wounded arm. That is all at present, so good-bye.

– Jim

Heroism Everywhere

After the July 1st offensive, it took weeks for the full extent of what happened at the Battle of Beaumont Hamel to become fully known. Among the initial reports from the battlefront were the following:

Captain James Allan Ledingham, the youngest captain, led his company in the charge. He was hit by enemy fire three times before he fell. Then he crawled, dragging himself into a shell hole where he remained for five hours. After hearing the moaning of a comrade, he pulled himself up to peek over the edge of his shelter and saw just a few yards from him an old friend, Lieutenant S. Robertson.[26]

Hardly able to move himself, Ledingham crawled to the aid of Robertson and under a rain of enemy fire, managed to hoist him onto his back to begin a lengthy and excruciating crawl towards help. The Captain's heroic effort was successful and he made it to the safety of the British lines where medics provided immediate help. Captain Ledingham was killed on October 17, 1917, at Passchendaele, during the Battle of the Somme.

Lt. Frost

Lt. S. Frost had been a bank clerk from Nova Scotia before the war. When the Regiment was under heavy fire from enemy machine guns, Frost went out, from the comparative safety of his trench, to rescue wounded comrades. He succeeded in bringing all three to safety and was heading back to rescue two others who had suffered multiple hits, when he was hit by a hail of enemy fire and died on his back.

---

[26] Lt. S. Robertson's name is not listed among those who fought with the Newfoundland Regiment in WWI. He was likely a member of one of the other Battalion's in the 88th Brigade.

Four Days Suffering

An article from London published July 12, 1916, in the *Evening Telegram,* described the four day ordeal of an unnamed private. It reported:

> In the charge was a young private who but an hour or so before the attack went into the firing line for the first time. He went over the parapet with his comrades and was probably one of those who got nearest to the German lines. All his comrades were shot down, and he fell into a shell hole filled with dead. He had no idea of the direction; he could not tell which were the German and which were the British lines. For four days he stayed there, shells exploding all round him and bullets coming apparently from all quarters if he as much as showed his nose.

> His rations were soon exhausted, and he had to take food and water from the dead around him. At the end of the fourth day, he determined to make for the trenches, but which direction he did not know. By good fortune, he chose the right direction and was taken in by a British patrol. He was quite unconcerned with regard to his adventure and the only explanation he gave was, 'Oh, I was fed up with it.'

The military brass spent exhaustive hours planning strategy, discussing and moving pins around on a map to show troop locations. Later historians would record the victories, losses, and describe the day to day progress and horrors of the war. But the reality was that it was men like Jim and Bert and the Carew brothers on the battlefield, ready to kill or be killed, frightened and exhausted, but courageous enough to try and dodge the bullets, bombs and enemy bayonets, upon whom the success of each battle depended. These soldiers were not responsible for the strategies and battle plans, good or bad, but they paid the supreme penalty when the strategists erred. This is the fact that made every one of them heroes.

Newfoundland Government Disappointed Blue Puttees

In October 1918, the surviving Blue Puttees were given leave to return to Newfoundland for a vacation from the battlefronts of

Europe. As the end of their leave approached, a public petition was circulated asking the Governor to approve an extension of their leave. The petition reflected widespread public support.

The prayer of the petition pointed out that in view of the outstanding contribution the Blue Puttees made at Gallipoli and in the Battle of the Somme, and the fact that "our boys" had not spent a Christmas at home in three years, that their leave be extended until after the Christmas season. It was an emotional issue that sparked some letters to the press including a poem by Jimmy Murphy, who often worked together with Johnny Burke, the Bard of Prescott Street.[27]

The poem follows:
"To the Blue Puttees
(A Plea to His Excellency for the extension of their furlough)"
By James Murphy

When Thor's trumpet sounded,
when fear and her minions
Lay locked in the breasts of some
nerve wanting youth.
Then courage unloosened her spotless
bright pinions,
and soon to her side rushed
five hundred recruits.

It is easy to bask neath the sun of contentment,
When peace with her white wings
fair freedom enjoys.
When sighted the first to uphold her
resentment,
We are proud to admit was her
Blue Puttee Boys.

They rose like the Phoenix, when
fresh from her ashes,
She illumes all the place that

---

[27] Jimmy Murphy, was as well known around old St. John's as his best friend Johnny Burke, and he wrote, as many, if not more, poems than Burke. Most of Murphy's poetry and songs were published in the newspapers over several decades.

lay darkened before.
It was so with those youths with
their life-moistened lashes,
Who showed to the world they
were true to the core.
They came at her call as a brother
meets brother,
With the love light of freedom imbued
in their eyes.
They went as if raised by a famed
Spartan mother,
Now, who fought more brave than
the Blue Puttee Boys.

O'er four years ago they left here
with our blessings
As pure as the dew which the
mountain rose sips;
They proved that for courage they are
the quintessence
And they sought not for praise from
Appollo's sweet lips.
Since then Hunnish Kultur, they have
helped to kill it.
They fought for the right against
oppression and lies,
And old Terra Nova today has
conceded,
That she fondly loves all her
Blue Puttee Boys.

They fought on the shores where the
Turk shows the Crescent.
Their requiems are sung by the
blue rolling waves.
Their courage in Flanders was never once lessened
Where France's fair lily blooms
over their graves.
While here with us now, are the
last that's remaining

Of that gallant band whom
the whole country prize.
We hope their request, they will
be obtaining,
For we know you deserve it
Brave Blue Puttee Boys.[28]

The petition was considered by the Governor and Sir Michael
Cashin and his cabinet, and it was turned down. The Governor told
the disappointed Blue Puttees, "It would be a breach of faith with
the Army Council which sent back a considerable number of men
from the Regiment for a period of rest to their own country." Both
the public and the Blue Puttees were disappointed by the decision.

---

[28] The Evening Telegram, October 4, 1918, p4.

Chapter 6

THE GREAT EXPERIMENT AT CAMBRAI

Regiment Reinforced after Losses

By July 28th sufficient reinforcements arrived in France to fill the depleted ranks of the Newfoundland Regiment which enabled them to move on to the next stage in the Battle of the Somme at Ypres. In addition to strengthening the defences there, the Newfoundlanders spent much time manning the front line at Hellfire Corner. By September 1915 the British were able to supply its forces fighting in the Somme with enough shells for the artillery to fire rolling barrages, enabling the infantry to move on to their own objectives. Germans had little time to man their machine guns as they had effectively done in the Battle of Beaumont Hamel.

On October 8th, the Regiment departed for Gueudecourt where they again faced the enemy in battle. By then the Battle of the Somme was fiercely raging and in its fourth month.

The British had still not taken Beaumont Hamel although they had gained five miles in the centre of the Front. A new battle was shaping up for the 29th Division near Gueudecourt on October 12th where the Newfoundland Regiment made it to the edge of that village. They were forced back a short distance after the regiments on both flanks failed to hold the line. The Newfoundlanders held their line against repeated counterattacks by the enemy until the next day when they were relieved. At this point the Newfoundlanders were facing Germany's famous Iron Division, a title earned through their record of being consistently strong in battle. Their original objective, Grease Trench, one of a series of trenches along the Somme, was captured on October 27th. The Newfoundland Regiment occupied and courageously defended this trench which today is the site of the Caribou Memorial.

When the Germans mounted a strong offensive to recover these lost positions, the 29th Division dug in to protect the ground so many had sacrificed their lives to gain. During this five month battle, the Newfoundlanders were in the front line near Lesboeufs. Heavy enemy shelling resulted in continuing Newfoundland casualties until the Regiment was relieved on November 22nd, and they were able to spend Christmas resting at nearby Camp en Amienois.

Newfoundlanders take 800 Prisoners

Following the Christmas break, the Regiment, as part of the 88th Brigade, moved to Le Transloy behind Sailly-Saillisel. The German Front ran south-eastward from this position. In the days that followed they took 800 German prisoners of which seventy-two were captured by CSM Gardiner whose amazing story is told in chapter seven.

During February 1917, while on the front line, near Sailly-Saillisel, Captain Leo Murphy wrote:

> Alex Reader has been killed by a sniper. He had been scooping out the section of the trench and a German sniper watched his head and shovel arising above the parapet from time to time and eventually "got"him. Sgt. Lever brought me his pay-book, the letters, the private expressions of his opinions, the Testament, carefully treasured from St. John's to Gallipoli and brought to France. 'I am in a dugout. If I should die, think only this of me...'

It is a voice from the dead. It is Alex Reader's voice, whose fine manly form was with me in the traverse only a few hours ago. The letters are sealed, the Testament is closed, the few personal souvenirs are wrapped up to go to Battalion headquarters.[1]

The Germans fought hard and heavy to regain ground loss but without success. A letter written home by a Cpl. W. Tobin indicated the hardship, frustration and suffering of the men in the trenches. The letter written on March 2, 1917, stated:

> Detailed with four men who were holding a strong point. We have a barricade 120 yards up the trench so we are a safe distance from his (enemy) egg bombs. Had to stand to with bayonets fixed all night. Spent worse night of my life in that trench, being cold, hungry, and fed up. I was ankle deep in icy mud all night. Very little going on in the way of shell fire but always expecting hell to let loose at any moment. Very pleased to see the light of day. A shell landed square in my

---

[1]Dr. David Facey-Crowther, editor, <u>Better Than The Best, The Royal Newfoundland Regiment</u>.

bombing post. I don't know how I escaped. My guardian angel was certainly looking after me.[2]

On April 9, 1917, the Canadian Corps captured Vimy Ridge in France which was the start of the offensive at Arras. The 29th Division, which the Newfoundland Regiment was part of, was assigned to attack along the Arras to Cambrai Road which was west of Arras at Monchy le Preux.

Corporal W. Tobin gave a glimpse into the life of a soldier at that time. He recalled:

On April 3, on way to Monchy. Spent the afternoon looking for something to eat. Money is not a great deal of good in a small French village where there are a number of troops. Had a fine nights rest in a hay loft. The rats are great playmates. We spent a good time banging tins at them in the dark.[3]

The Regimental Chaplin, Father Tom Nangle, delivering a lecture on the Newfoundland Regiment later in St. John's, told an audience:

Silly, Silly, Sal. (Sailly-Saillisee). Time after time the Germans crept up to the trench and bombed it. They finally got into the trench and drove the boys along it for forty yards. Gerald Byrne seized a bucket of bombs and, shouting to the boys to follow, started along the trench. The boys did follow. They drove the Germans, not only from the forty yards which they had taken from the Newfoundlanders, but also another sixty yards of their own and more than that, the Newfoundlanders held the whole one hundred yards.[4]

Monchy

The start of the battle at Monchy did not go well for the Newfoundland and Essex Regiments who began the attack from

---

[2] Ibid.
[3] Ibid.
[4] Ibid.

trenches just outside Monchy. They passed the front line German trenches with little opposition and were moving along the Somme towards Infantry Hill. Here, the Germans surprised them by launching an attack from two wooded areas which surrounded both regiments. Overwhelmed by the numbers of Germans, many surrendered and were taken prisoners.

At Division Headquarters in Monchy, there was confusion. Intelligence had been received that startled the senior officers. Reports said that the Germans were advancing to the trenches left earlier that morning by two Regiments. The German advance put them in a position to take Monchy. This possibility was a real shocker to the Generals. One said that if Monchy is taken by the Germans, it will take 40,000 troops to recapture it.

This marked a critical point in the battle, and the slightest indecision could have resulted in defeat. With reserve forces two hours away, one senior officer took a risky initiative. Lt. Col. James Forbes-Robertson, second in command of the Newfoundland Regiment, put together a raiding force of twenty men from Headquarters and attempted to lead them to a hedge outside the village. Ten men reached the hedge with Forbes-Robertson. Through sheer courage and determination, along with their skilful handling of machine guns, they succeeded in stopping the German advance into Monchy.

During this battle, forty Germans were shot, thirty of these being hit by the fire from Forbes-Robertson's gun. This little band of soldiers held off the Germans until reserves arrived about two hours later. Father Tom Nangle noted, "Forbes-Robertson and the party of ten men established themselves in the grove and held off the Germans all day."[5]

Although Lt. Colonel Forbes-Robertson was not a Newfoundlander, he had been second-in-command of the Royal Newfoundland Regiment since 1916. He was awarded the Victoria Cross for his heroism in battle. The name of James Forbes-Robertson and the men that saved Monchy that day are inscribed on a plaque on the wall of the bunker on which the Caribou Memorial rests.[6]

---

[5] Forgotten Heroes, a publication of the Royal Newfoundland Regiment, 1981.
[6] The unit that saved the day for the British Forces consisted of: Lt. Col. Forbes-Robertson, Captain K. Keegan, Lt. A. Rose, Staff-Sgt. J.J. Hillier, Sgts. C. Parsons and R. Walterfield, Corporal J. Hounsel, Private W. Pitcher, Private F.Curran.

About ten days later, the Newfoundland Regiment, with depleted forces, was in action again. On April 23rd, they participated in an attack down the Arras-Cambrai road. They had just left a farm when the Germans launched their counterattack, but the Newfoundlanders were able to stop them. During this battle the Regiment's doctor earned the Military Cross through his heroic efforts in attending to the injured under gunfire.

Newfoundlanders Held at Reprisal Camps

It was not an easy task locating soldiers who were taken as POWs. During the defence of Monchy, 150 Newfoundlanders were surrounded by 500 German fighters and taken as prisoners of war. For the remainder of the war some were harshly treated by their captors. History notes that at this time in the war, the Germans were angered by Britain's delay in responding to a request to move all German POWs to a point no less than thirty kilometres behind the firing line.

The Germans retaliated by advising that all British prisoners taken in the future would be held as Prisoners of Reprisal and subject to the following punishment:

Very short of food, no beds, plenty of hard work, also to be very near the German guns under English shellfire. They are to receive no pay for working, no soap for washing or shaving, no baths; no boots to wear. Everything we can possibly do to harm and injure all English Prisoners of Reprisal will be done by the German Military Command.[7]

The Germans provided writing materials to the prisoners and instructed them to write home to public officials and tell them of the terrible treatment they were receiving. The harsh treatment was to last until the British acceded to the German request, after which the English POWs would be transferred to prison camps in Germany where they would be well treated.

The Newfoundlanders were held at a Reprisal Camp in an old fort outside Lille, France for more than four weeks. The cells were

---

[7] G.W Nicholson, The Fighting Newfoundlander, p362.

damp and measured thirty by ten feet. 100 prisoners were crowded into each cell. They were forced to sleep on stone floors or wooden boards. Reduced rations were given to them during this period.

In the morning they had; one cup of brewed from burnt beans. At noon they were given one slice of black bread and a bowl of watered down cabbage soup. Helmets were used as soup bowls and no utensils were given out. For supper, one Newfoundlander noted, "We got a good meal of nothing at all, which was as good as change." In just four weeks the men were so physically worn down that they could hardly walk.

From the Reprisal Camp, Newfoundlanders were spread out in prison camps in Germany, Belgium, and Poland. Twenty-five men had died as German POWs. One prisoner, Private Moyle T. Stick escaped a POW camp in Prussia and made it safely to Norway. Stick was awarded the Military Medal for his services to his country. He was the only Newfoundland POW to escape captivity.

Conditions for the POWs did improve a little when they were transferred. The food was terrible, but it was a time when the German people themselves were on the verge of starvation. Prisoners snuck outside camps to steal vegetables from peasants' gardens and their food was supplemented somewhat when the Red Cross delivered packages from home.

Lieutenant Sandy Baird recalled in a letter home that all the prisoners looked forward to getting packages from home including "hardtack" which was made in St. John's by Harvey & Co. Hardtack is still popular among Newfoundlanders today and is used to make fish 'n brewis or just brewis.

The War Contingent Association made sure that a fourteen-pound parcel of food was sent regularly to individual prisoners, once the address was known. When the war was drawing to a close and the Germans realized they were losing, the POWs were treated much better.

Missing in Action Turn up as POWs

An important independent source of information on conditions inside the German POW camps in 1915 and 1916 came from the United States Embassy in Berlin at a time in the war when the Americans were still neutral. However, the Germans suspended that privilege in 1916. According to the *Evening Telegram*, August 1916:

> Dr. Steward Irwin of John Hopkins University returned to New York yesterday on the Scandinavian-American liner *Hellig Claw* after spending five months in Germany inspecting prison camps. He said he found a very strong anti-American feeling in Germany and that finally the Reichstag refused to permit him to visit any more camps.
>
> Among the 3,000,000 prisoners he said, there are about 500,000 English military men. We were allowed to talk to the men but individual examinations were refused. In one hospital we saw men in the last stages of tuberculosis whose cases were designated as pneumonia. In one camp I saw prisoners storing away food for future use because a shortage of supplies was expected.
>
> The English prisoners were permitted to receive boxes of food from home but the French and Russian were not.

What the Americans Found

The Germans acknowledged having received complaints in some camps about the food but explained that this was often due to the size and variety of the nationals occupying a camp.

For example, at Doberitz POW camp there were 8000 prisoners of which 3600 were British. The camp menu had to consider the majority in the camp which meant an all around mixed menu. The cooks were Russians, Indians, and French.

In respect to complaints of work, all British soldiers, including Newfoundlanders, were called upon to do only their share in fatigue work. The Dobertiz prison was a superior structure compared to most other German prisons because it had been built to house German soldiers but when the need arose was converted into a POW camp. Due to the large size of its rooms, the prison did not have a mess, and the men were expected to use their rooms for eating, sleeping and recreation. This was the situation that existed in 1915 when the American Ambassador to Berlin visited the German POW camp and compiled his report.

The Ambassadors report stated:

The British are a minority among the prisoners and in respect to food etc the majority of different races have to be considered. Consequently, less attention to the British way of life and wishes than is possible where only one race is considered. No authentic case of bad treatment has been found in any of the camps visited yet.[8]

John B. Jackson, a British official who accompanied the American Ambassador, reported to the British Government from Berlin on March 31, 1915, "...as far as I have been able to ascertain, there is no discrimination against officers and soldiers."

All was not as rosy in some other camps inspected. In these camps, POWs were treated more like ordinary criminals than officer POWs. Guards were often rough in their handing of prisoners. Many camps failed to provide special accommodations for senior officers. The latrines were not constructed on drains and barely sufficient to meet camp needs. Officers were required to pay from their monthly payments 1.50 marks per day for their food, and bathing was permitted only once per week.[9]

Every effort was made in the camps to accommodate the religious needs of prisoners. In cases where military chaplains were lacking, Protestant and Catholic clergy were brought into the prisons from nearby communities. In the case of Indian prisoners, live sheep were supplied to kill in accordance with their religious rights.

One of the largest POW camps in Germany was Zossen, which was housed almost 16,000 POWs. This was built outside a village in an area surrounded by pine woods and some rivers and ponds. The menu was changed each day, with beef being served on Mondays, Wednesdays, and Thursdays, and pork was given on Sundays. There was no meat for the other days.

At the Gottingen prison, which housed 6000 POWs, the prisoners organized libraries with help from the professors and pastors from the nearby village. They also had a camp orchestra and choir.

---

[8] PANL GN 2-14 Box 3, File #18.
[9] The British paid their officers serving in POW camps one dollar per day which was handled through the American Embassy in Berlin until the U.S entered the war in 1917.

After several of the Somme battles, many prisoners were taken to hospitals at Cologne for treatment. When visited by the Ambassador's party, there was not one prisoner who had a complaint over their treatment. All prisoners needing vaccines were given then, and the recovery rate among those injured was good.[10]

After Monchy

After Monchy in 1917, the Regiment, with their numbers considerably reduced was sent to a quit area behind the lines for rest and relaxation. This was followed by training at a place called the Bool Ring (Bull Ring) near the village of Rouen. This was a centre which provided hard and rigorous traiing for new troops and those getting ready to go to battle. When their training ended, they were moved out on June 27th to Ypres Salient where they occupied trenches along the Yser Canal, east of Ypres. The day by day horrors of war resumed when the battle continued. On July 10, 1917, Private Andrew Parsons wrote home:

> A small shell fell on the other side of my chum and beat him into the mud and water. He was covered with blood. He was dead. I had no one to help me and talk about home and the old pals of home and the time we would have when we get back. It was not very good around Hellfire Corner sometimes, it was not long before I knew what war was.[11]

Lt. L. Woods wrote from France in July 1917:

> I had no sooner landed here in France for the second time, then I had to arrange for a Church Parade. We held the parade in a wood not far from the line. It is strange to be singing hymns to the accompaniment of artillery and the other sounds of war.[12]

The Third Battle of Ypres continued all summer and developed into the Battle of Passchendaele. The lengthy

---

[10] PANL GN2-14 Box 3.
[11] Ibid.
[12] Dr. David Facey-Crowther, <u>Better than the Best. The Newfoundland Regiment</u>.

Passchendaele Ridge on the Somme was of strategic importance to the British whose plan was to use it as a base of departure for a rapid further advance. From holding a defensive position, the 29th Division with the Newfoundland Regiment initiated two major assaults against the Germans.

On August 16, 1917, the 29th started at Steenbeek Stream while the Newfoundland Regiment, with other battalions, headed out across mud and swamp adjacent east of the railway line leading towards their target at Broembeek Stream, a stepping stone closer to Passchendaele Ridge. They destroyed the enemy pill boxes[13] in the area to make way for their advance. All their major objectives were achieved. The wounded were taken from the battlefield to the hospital nearby in Etaples. On August 13th the German planes bombed the hospital, and Private J. Walsh, one of the wounded housed there was killed.

The Newfoundland Regiment was relieved after this success and for the next two months they moved back to defensive positions at a place called Cannes Farm. On October 9th, they were back on the attack and once again achieved their objective following a battle in an area of rough terrain.

Torrential Rainfalls
The two co-authors of *Marching to Armageddon* gave a graphic description of the weather that added to the misery the troops faced in those October battles. They stated:

The rains returned, driving, drenching torrents that restored the churned soil to an endless sea of stinking mud, spotted with the bodies of horses, men and all the detritus of war. Wounded drowned in it. When eight or a dozen stretcher-bearers were needed to move a single casualty, too few reached hospitals. For the first time,

---

[13] The Pill Boxes referred to were small concrete structures from which the enemy launched machine gun attacks on advancing troops.

Newfoundlanders getting ready for Battle of Cambrai-1917. (PANL)

Germans found British soldiers eager to surrender and talking of killing their officers.[14]

The two battles won by the Newfoundlanders were the Battle of the Steenbeek and the Battle of the Broembeek which were part of the larger offensive aimed at capturing Passchendaele Ridge. The Newfoundland Regiment was building a reputation for courage in battle that was earning it respect throughout the Allied military and in London. The Regiment, as part of the 29th Division, was successful in gaining control of all the objectives in both confrontations. These were their only successes on October 9th. Just a few days before, some British troops were frustrated enough to consider surrender because things had gone so badly.

Preparing for Cambrai

By mid-November, the Newfoundland Regiment was at Peronne, France and training continually in preparation for a battle which immortalized their memory, the Battle of Cambrai. The book of *The Royal Newfoundland Regiment* noted:

---

[14] Desmond Morton and J. Granatstein, <u>Marching to Armageddon</u>, p174.

This was the great experiment which deployed Tanks to break the Hindenberg Line. The 88th Brigade advanced from Gouzencourt, accompanied by tanks. They passed the first line of defence of the Hindenberg Line and the support line, the main German defences before Cambrai. The Newfoundland Regiment, as part of the 88th Brigade, advanced to Marcoing Copse[15] and the Canal. Fire from across the canal held them up until a tank came up and poured heavy fire into the enemy strong point. The Newfoundlanders rushed across the lock on the canal and established a bridgehead on the opposite bank. This was expanded and the Regiment advanced to Marcoing, then to Masnieres, where they held the line.

For a long time after, the Newfoundland Regiment referred to their part in the Battle of Cambrai as the Battle of Marcoing and Masnieres,[16] which were German held areas on the march to Cambrai.

The Grand Experiment

British born Brigadier General Hugh Tudor, who later became a permanent resident of Newfoundland, was a brilliant military strategist whose ideas were the basis for the overall strategy which became an experiment in warfare in the Battle of Cambrai. The British Military held high expectations for what history described as the 'grand experiment.'

Tudor broke with conventional war practices by recommending the use of "a surprise attack." Previously, the enemy was forewarned of an attack when the artillery units began firing towards their location by "trial and error" to measure the exact location to gage their artillery guns. Once the artillery unit had fixed the distance, it would launch the actual bombardment of enemy positions to clear the way for the infantry to advance. However, the practice alerted the enemy that an infantry attack was pending. To solve this problem, Tudor replaced this preliminary ranging with the surveying rules used in adjusting

---

[15] A small group of trees near the canal.
[16] Forgotten Heroes, published by Royal Newfoundland Regiment, 1981.

Winston Churchill's invention, the war tank, was introduced into WWI against his wishes. He felt that there should have been more manufactured before being used in the war. (IWA)

calculations due to weather changes. This enabled the artillery to withhold their fire until the start of the infantry advance.

Tudor was supported by General H. J. Ellis, Commanding Officer of the Tank Corp, in advocating the use of tanks as part of his battle strategy.[17]

The success of Tudor's ideas depended on the employment of a large number of tanks breaking through the traditional wire defences and clearing the way for the infantry. When these broke through enemy lines, a large scale cavalry attack would follow through and assault the main target.

The Winnie Tank

Russian author, Leon Trotsky, once said:

It is common place in military history that there exists continuity between the closing of one war and the opening phase of the next: the weapons and the ideas invented or formed toward the end of one armed conflict dom-inate the first stage of the next conflict.

---

[17] Colonel G.W.L. Nicholson, The Fighting Newfoundlander.

The Newfoundland Battalion marching through Berneville, France, May 9, 1917. (PANL)

This is true of an invention by Winston Churchill which he named the 'land battle-ship' later known as the 'tank 'while serving as Lord of the Admiralty in World War I.[18]

Churchill's invention was meant for the army and when Balfour replaced him as Lord of the Admiralty and Churchill was forced to resign in the middle of the war, he criticized his predecessor for involving himself in a project better suited for the army.[19]

---

[18] Captain B. H. Liddell Hart claimed in his book The Real War published in 1930 that, although a British Royal Commission had dealt with the issue of who invented the tank, others were still making claim to that honour.
[19] Churchill was invited back into the cabinet in 1917.

Major General Sir Hugh Tudor on the left with Belgium's King Albert inspecting Royal Newfoundland Regiment. (IWM)

Balfour ordered that the project be stopped, and those "Winnie Tanks," as they were dubbed, which had been finished be put into immediate use. Balfour argued that the development and responsibility for tanks was more appropriate for the army rather than the navy which had been Churchill's responsibility.

Churchill opposed introducing the tank into battle at that time and suggested the invention was not yet ready. However, his objections were ignored, and the "Winnies" were sent into action. On September 15, 1916, a handful of them went into operation at the Somme and in November they played a key role at Cambrai. Churchill said, "My poor 'land battleships' have been left off prematurely on a petty scale."[20]

The Winnie was successful and became an established army vehicle by WWII.

After the war, when several people were claiming to have invented the "tank," the British Parliament appointed an enquiry to determine which claim was valid. It concluded that Winston Churchill was the inventor and should be recognized as the patent owner. Churchill declined the offer and noted that it was part of the work he had done as a servant of the Crown.

---

[20] William Manchester, <u>The Last Lion</u>.

A German Prisoner surrendering at The Battle of Cambrai after which the Newfoundland +Regiment became The Royal Newfoundland Regiment. (IWM)

Tudor's Connection with St. John's

In 1920 Sir Hugh Tudor became commander of the infamous British Black and Tans, named after the colours in their uniform. They were sent to Ireland to combat the lawlessness developing from the increasing demands for independence. Due to the shortage of appropriate police uniforms for the group, mostly veterans of the Great War, they were issued khaki military uniforms with black belts. In Ireland Tudor commanded the Irish Constabulary, the Dublin Police and the Black and Tans.[21]

Oral history in St. John's claims that following the episode in Ireland, Tudor spent some time in Scotland and then settled in Newfoundland to escape the retribution of the Irish Republican Army. According to this claim, the IRA sent men to St. John's to assassinate Tudor, but only the intervention of a Catholic priest kept the order from being carried out.

I did speak with the late James Byrne, a St. John's businessman, who never hid his sympathies and support for the IRA and who claimed that other prominent men of the city shared his views. Byrne was convinced the story is true, and added that Tudor had been tried-in- absentia by the IRA for what they described as his "...crimes against the Irish," for which he was sentenced to be executed.

---

[21] Jack Fitzgerald, Jack Fitzgerald's Notebook.

Tudor's wartime connections with many Newfoundlanders in France may have played a role in his coming to Newfoundland. Sir Hugh Tudor passed away in 1965 at the age of ninety-five. He died at the Veteran's Pavilion at the old General Hospital in the east end of St. John's.

Major Role for Regiment

The Newfoundland Regiment played a major role in the Battle of Cambrai 1917. The success of the whole operation depended on the troops of the 29th Division, of which the Newfoundland Battalion was a part, in securing the villages of Masnieres and Marcoing and establishing a strong bridgehead on the far side of the St. Quentin Canal.

Once their objective was achieved, five cavalry divisions were to pass through the newly secured areas to capture Cambrai, Bourlon Wood on an adjacent hill on the left flank, and then cross the Sensee River on the north end of Cambrai. Upon completion of this operation four corps in reserve would move in to secure the entire area of Cambrai and the area bounded by the Sensee River and the Canals.[22]

At 6:20 a.m. on November 20th, literally without warning, the British stormed the German position. The enemy was taken completely by surprise. The massive effort saw hundreds of British aircraft roaring over the German line, strafing trenches with bombs; 378 tanks thundered forward, flattening barbed wire; the infantry of five divisions followed on a five mile front. A thousand hidden guns opened fire for the first time, overwhelming selected targets with shells and poison gas. The German soldiers were shocked and overwhelmed.

The tank, the new weapon of war, terrorized German troops. Military historian G. W. Nicholson described their reaction at the trenches:

> The Germans watched with terror the long line of iron monsters plunging down upon them through the gloom of a fog filled dawn, spitting fire from their machine-guns and smashing down the wire entanglements in their path. Then they were upon them, flattening machine-gun posts

---

[22] G.W. Nicholson, The Fighting Newfoundlander.

crew and all, and turning to sweep the length of the
trenches with their fire. The unusual width of the trenches
proved no serious obstacle to the tanks, which dropped
enormous bundles of tightly-bound brushwood, each
weighing a ton and a half, into the gap to assist their
crossing.

In anticipation of a possible tank attack, the Germans had a
double line of deep trenches 250 yards apart and each one was
twelve feet wide with the top built up to stop or slow down the
advance of tanks. This was reinforced behind with a support line
made up of a barbed-wire front with more trenches at the rear
edge of the battle zone. Five thousand yards behind this was the
"Siegfried Line", which comprised another system of trenches.
The British used a different name for the Siegfried. To them it
was "The Masnieres-Beaurevoir Line."[23]
Following the new weapon of war were waves of foot soldiers
who were rounding up German prisoners. Six-thousand Germans,
mostly shell-shocked, surrendered without resistance. Despite this
massive effort, by the end of the day, the British had advanced only
three or four miles. The battle was far from over, and the Germans
had surprises of their own.
By sunset the next day, the Newfoundlanders were on the
outskirts of Cambrai. Their fellow units joined them in securing
the village of Marcoing and they dug in on the far-side of the Canal
with the Newfoundlanders. However, things changed when
German reinforcements arrived from the Russian Front, and the
British planned attack on the enemy's rear defence was cancelled.
The British tank force was rendered almost useless. Tanks
were broken down, damaged and left on the battlefield. The plan
to use the Cavalry Corps as a force in the battle was halted by
German machine gun attacks. Haig's army was decimated, and on
December 1st, the German ace Manfred von Richthofen's
squadron of low-flying planes led a German counterattack.[24]

---

[23] Morton and Granatstein, <u>Marching to Armageddon</u>.
[24] Ibid.

Earning the prefix "Royal"

When the Germans launched a major counterattack on December 30th, the Newfoundland Regiment with other units of the 29th Division responded with one of the most effective delaying actions along the entire British line that day. Private Pike recalled that Captain Bartlett called out, "Come on the Boo," the "Boo" short for Caribou, and the Newfoundlanders launched a spirited confrontation with the Germans.

The Newfoundlanders were in the advance guard and heavy shelling almost wiped them out. During this battle, seventy-nine men were killed, 340 wounded, and forty-three were missing when the fight stopped. The Newfoundlanders moved up and down the trenches firing randomly to deceive the enemy into believing they were a much larger force.

The German counterattack was relentless, but despite the desperateness of their situation, the 29th Division held their position. The next day, with a remarkable demonstration of will and courage, they successfully held off nine separate attacks by the Germans. It was not until darkness on the second day of their unflagging resistance that the Division was forced to withdraw.

Horror on Battlefield

During this withdrawal, a mystery developed on the battlefield. A company of the Newfoundland Regiment suddenly came under heavy fire which pinned them down. This attack was mysterious because all German machine guns and presence in the area had been destroyed, and there was no apparent explanation for the attack. Lt. Gerald Whitty, who earned the Military Cross that day, accompanied by another officer set out on a mission to trace the source of gunfire. What they found was an unexpected horror.

A British soldier in the doorway of a partially destroyed armoured tank was firing his gun indiscriminately at anyone or anything moving within sight. Whitty engaged the man in conversation in an attempt to persuade him to drop his gun and surrender. During the exchange, Whitty learned that the man was deranged from the horror he and his tank crew had just encountered. The armoured tank had new battlefront horrors that soldiers were to experience when hit by enemy explosives. This particular tormented soldier witnessed the terrifying deaths of

his fellow crew members and experienced the dreadful heat inside
the tank when German shells struck it. Half his face was shot away
by enemy gunfire. While the soldier struggled to converse with
Whitty, he was mercifully killed instantly by enemy fire.[25]

High Praise for Newfoundland Regiment

Major General D. E. Cayley, who headed the 88th Brigade, was
impressed with the Newfoundlanders at Cambrai. He said, "Their
grand defence and counter attack at the Battle of Cambrai was
truly worthy of them." Field Marshall Douglas Haig described the
Regiment's performance as, "...worthy of the best traditions of the
British Army."[26]

Having experienced the rain and mud of Gallipoli, the
Newfoundlanders were ready for what faced them at the start of
the Battle of Cambrai. In the first stage of the battle, they were to
advance from Pilckem Ridge to the village of Broembeek, on the
left of the first wave of attack, across a battlefield that presented a
real challenge. The entire area was a low-lying, marshy field which
had been devastated by shell-fire. A continuous rainfall which
lasted more than two weeks turned the field into a swamp. Yet,
these Newfoundlanders were determined and persistent, despite
their struggle with the elements which slowed their advance
considerably. Senior officers were more than pleased that under
such adverse conditions they achieved their objectives on
schedule.

Fighting in the Swamp

On September 11, 1917, the following item in the *Montreal Star*
described how Newfoundland soldiers persevered in overcoming
the 'swamp' obstacle to win a battle. The headline stated:
NEWFOUNDLANDERS TAKE FORT. The article read:

> It was a 'floating swamp' that stretched over five hundred
> yards, just beyond Steenbeeck, and at the end of it was the
> heavily fortified enemy position. It was a quaking morass
> which gives no foothold anywhere and the men found that

---

[25] Colonel W.L. Nicholson, The Fighting Newfoundlander, p410.
[26] Dr. David Facey-Crowther, Better Than the Best, p41.

it varied in depth. When a man sank much above his waist, he had to stay there to be pulled out, if fortune favoured later. Those only knee high or waist high went in the swamp and went on even though the swamp was being swept by machine gunfire.

Among them, Newfoundlanders, trappers and lumbermen, all accustomed to fight nature in all her moods. They went doggedly on into the gray of early morning, wading, stumbling, forcing their way the best they could. Those who were hit badly sank into the ooze.

Some slightly wounded went after their comrades or made their way back, but the rest went on with their rifles held above their heads, panting and almost worn out. On the heels of the barrage, they rushed the great fort. There was a short burst of wild fighting, and the front was theirs after as fine an exhibition of mere physical endurance as men have ever been called upon to show.

When it was over, they helped their comrades, still embedded in the slime, and in bodies of three or four, they pulled them out and got them safely to solid ground.[27]

Newfoundland was the source of supply for "sphagnum moss"[28] which was used by hospitals near the battlefront to dress wounds. The appeal to the Governor of Newfoundland, the day after the battle, read: "Send sphagnum moss to troops. Urgently needed in hospitals for surgical dressings." The request was treated as a priority, and a supply of the moss was quickly shipped.

The outstanding performance of the Newfoundland Regiment in the Battle of Cambrai brought them surprising recognition in January 1918. His Majesty, King George V, bestowed the grant of the title "Royal" to the Regiment. This was an honour that had occurred only twice before in wartime history; the first was in 1665 and the second was in 1885. It also marked the only time a

---

[27] PANL MG439 Box 1 File 12.

[28] Sphagnum moss, is defined by the Oxford Dictionary as, "Any various pale or ashy mosses of the genus Sphagnum whose decomposed remains form peat.

regiment of the British Army was awarded the title "Royal" during WWI while fighting still continued. A second honour bestowed upon the Regiment after Cambrai was having the word 'Cambrai' emblazoned on the Regimental Colours.

The victory at Cambrai may have brought a quicker ending to the war if Haig had maintained the advantage his troops had won. Historian B. H. Liddell Hart provided the following assessment of the British strategy in his book *The Real War 1914-1918:*

> The folly of the last phase, from September 25, onwards, was that, the crest of the ridge and its commanding observation having at last been, won, the advantage was thrown away by fighting a way down into the valley beyond. Thereby, the troops were doomed to spend the winter in flooded trenches. 'Somme mud' was soon to be notorious. Thus the miscalled "Battles of the Somme" closed in an atmosphere of disappointment, and with such a drain on the British forces that the coincident strain of the enemy was obscured.

The Yanks are coming!

When the British destroyed transatlantic cable lines coming out of Germany early in the war, President Woodrow Wilson of the U. S. gave the Germans permission to use the American wireless transmission system. British intelligence was able to monitor messages going and coming out of Germany because of its access to telegraphic lines in North America. On January 16, 1917, the British intercepted a treacherous message from Germany's Foreign Minister to the German Ambassador in Mexico. He requested that Mexico enter the war on Germany's side and in return a German victory would give them New Mexico, Texas, and Arizona.

Shrewdly, the British held the message until they obtained a copy from the German Embassy in Mexico City which they later used to convince the Germans that there was an intelligence leak in the embassy. On February 26th, when they had this concrete piece of evidence, they officially passed it on to the American Embassy in London and waited for the consequences. Wilson allowed it to be released to the press, and it sparked outrage across the country.

German submarines sank three more American ships in late March. On April 6, 1917, at the request of their President, Congress declared war on Germany.[29]

The Germans launched another offensive in the Spring of 1918 which lasted throughout March, April and May. The Royal Newfoundland Regiment was called upon to join with the 34th Division to stem the attack of the enemy offensive. The Germans had advanced to within forty miles of Paris and threatened to cut off the British Army from its supply lines along the coast. Fortunately, the Germans ran out of men and supplies.

The Newfoundland Regiment found itself in a desperate defensive battle on April 10 that went on for the following ten days. They had formed a defensive line along the railway tracks near the Steenwerck Station facing south towards the advancing Germans. The Newfoundlanders held the position, but many men were killed or wounded in this effort. Their losses could not be replaced so they returned to a reserve area.

On April 29, 1918, in the final months of the war, the Royal Newfoundland Regiment left the 29th Division to take up an assignment to guard the Headquarters of Field Marshall Sir Douglas Haig at Montreuil. The departure was emotional for all present. As the Regiment passed the Divisional Commander, the band played, "Will Ye no'come back again."

Major General D. E. Cayley said:

In bidding good-bye to the Royal Newfoundland Regiment on their departure from the 29th Division, I wish to place on record my very great regret at their withdrawal from a division in which they have served so long and brilliantly. The whole of their active service since September 1915, has been performed in this division, and during all that time, the Battalion has shown itself to be under, all circumstances of good and bad fortune, a splendid fighting unit. At Suvla, Beaumont Hamel, Gueudecourt, Monchy, Cambrai and during the last fighting near Bailleul, they have consistently maintained the highest standards of fighting efficiency and determination. They

---

[29] Twentieth Century Almanac, 1918.

can look back on a record of which they and their fellow countrymen have every right to be proud.[30]

The Newfoundland Regiment was brought up to strength again by September 11, 1918, when they were attached to the 28th Brigade of the 9th Division. By then the German Offensive, suffering a lack of reinforcements and supplies, was exhausted. As part of the 9th Division, the Royal Newfoundland Regiment advanced as far as Hell Fire Corner near Ypres. On October 14th, the advance was halted by a German gun which pinned down the Regiment and inflicted many casualties. Three soldiers moved forward to take out the gun. They were: Lt. Newman, Sgt. Brazil and Private Thomas Ricketts. Ricketts ran back to get more ammunition for the Lewis Gun which he carried forward across no-man's-land. The risk and personal danger surrounding this effort resulted in Tommy Ricketts being awarded the Victoria Cross. His story is told in chapter seven.

The last attack for the Royal Newfoundland Regiment took place on October 20, 1918, at Beveran. Its last casualties occurred on October 25th and are buried at the British War Cemetery at Ingoyghem and Vichte in Belgium. The last Newfoundland soldier wounded during WWI was a Private Courage who was struck in the arm by shrapnel while working in the cookhouse at Gullenghem on October 30, 1918.

Newfoundland Regiment's Water Street Barracks 1918

When the Department of Militia took over administration of the Royal Newfoundland Regiment from the Newfoundland Patriotic Association in 1917, the Regiment was still without a military base for its soldiers. Troops were being billeted in private homes around St. John's and were using the CLB Armoury as headquarters. This changed during the summer and fall of 1918 when the Department secured quarters for the troops at the Curling Rink and the Prince's Rink in St. John's. The Department felt that this was important for the control and discipline of the soldiers.

At this time in 1918 the Military Service Act was passed, and the provision of suitable winter quarters for a large number of troops prompted the Department to approve a permanent barracks for

[30] Ibid.

the Regiment. As a result, the Militia Department purchased a large building located at 28-44 Water Street East, formerly occupied by the Empire Woodworking Factory, to convert into a barracks. It was still in use when the war ended on November 11, 1918, but had not reached its full capacity.

Meanwhile, during its short life, it was said to be very comfortable and most suitable in all respects for its purpose. When the war ended, and with the Spanish Flu spreading, these barracks became a hospital for the veterans of the war. It was later destroyed by fire.

After the November 11, 1918 Armistice, the Royal New-foundland Regiment marched across Belgium into Germany arriving there on December 4th. The Regiment stayed there as an Occupation Force until February 14th. They made it to London in time to participate in the Victory Parade on May 3, 1919, and were home in Newfoundland in time to mark the first 'July 1st Memorial Day.'

The Terrible Loss

In 1914, when the call went out throughout Newfoundland for volunteers, 12,425 men came forward to enlist. Six thousand one hundred and seventy-nine were accepted into the Newfoundland Regiment and an additional sixty-two joined them in Great Britain. The Regiment sent thirty-eight officers and 1,140 other ranks to serve in Gallipoli. When these men were moved to fight in France and Belgium, another 4,108 men and 105 officers joined them. Two thousand, three hundred and fourteen men were wounded, some more than once.

Taken as POWs were one 176 soldiers. Thirty-four of these died in German prison camps. The total number of fatalities was 1,305 men of all ranks. Many other Newfoundlanders died while serving in the British Navy. For decades after the war, Newfoundlanders wore blue poppies on Remembrance Day to honour their war dead.

On August 26, 1919, the 1st Newfoundland Battalion, The Royal Newfoundland Regiment; the 2nd (Reserve) Battalion, The Royal Newfoundland Regiment; and the Newfoundland Forestry Corps were officially disbanded.

Chapter 7

WARTIME COURAGE AND DARING

Best Sniper in the British Army

At a time in Colonial history when illiteracy was widespread, John Shiwak had taught himself to read and write. The fact that he accomplished this in the most northern area of Labrador, in an isolated Inuit community, makes his achievement even more amazing. In 1913 Lacey Amy, a Canadian journalist, had persuaded him to keep a diary which at the end of each winter supplied her with many stories about the life of natives in Labrador. She described Shiwak as a skilled writer who spoke from the heart "...in a thumbnail dash of words, he carried on straight into the clutch of the soundless Arctic."

Shiwak was also an adventurer, expert hunter and was a natural for recruitment into the Legion of Frontiersmen when they set up a unit in Labrador. His skills with a rifle became of great value when war broke out. The Patriotic Association of Newfoundland accepted an offer from Dr. Wilfred Grenfell to recruit volunteers, many of whom had already been trained in the Legion of Frontiersmen. Among the Grenfell recruits was John Shiwak. It didn't take long for him to earn respect among all ranks in the Royal Newfoundland Regiment.

While training in St. John's, Shiwak's expert marksman helped the Regiment win many shooting competitions, and it earned him a position as one of the Regiment's snipers. He was among the second reserve draft "F" Company which was sent overseas on June 20, 1915, on the HMT *Calgarian*.

By November 1916 he was in the midst of the famous Battle of Cambrai. This was the battle where some of General Hugh Tudor's new wartime techniques were being introduced for the first time. In November 1915, with the British making headway, the Germans added two extra divisions to their forces. One of these divisions had just returned from the Russian Front.

Some generals were alarmed by this move and gave serious consideration to halting the movement, already underway, of the Newfoundland Regiment (29th Division) toward its objective of Masnieres. However, after much debate, they decided to press on with their attack fully confident that they would defeat the Germans.

On November 20th at 11:30 a.m., the Newfoundland Regiment was moving along the canal which ran between Masnieres and Beaurevoir called the Siegfried II Line by the Germans. The Germans had destroyed an iron bridge across the canal which forced the Newfoundlanders to take another route. The area was under heavy German machine-gunfire. However, the Newfoundlanders marched along the canal hidden from enemy view by a high brick wall. A stray enemy shell went over the wall and struck in the centre of the column. Ten men were killed instantly and fifteen were wounded. One of those killed was the Inuk John Shiwak. Shiwak's Commanding Officer described him as, "The best sniper in the British Army."

Historian G. W. Nicholson wrote, "His loss was keenly felt throughout the Regiment for his matchless marksmanship and his skill as a scout and observer, together with his reliability and good nature, these had won him many friends."

His fellow soldiers continued on and made it to their objective at Masnieres where they remained as a counter-attack Battalion.

Journalist Lacey Amy in tribute to Shiwak wrote:

He had earned his long rest. Out there in lonesome Snipers' Land he lay, day after day; and the cunning that made him a hunter of fox, and marten, and otter, and bear, and wolf brought to him better game. And all he ever asked was: 'When will the war be over?' Only then would he return to his huskies and traps where few men dare a life of ice for a living almost as cold.'[1]

John Shiwak, the Inuit-Patriot, was laid to rest near the spot where he fell.

NL Soldiers Treated as Heroes in New York
To the *Evening Telegram*, June 1918
Report from New York:

Ten Newfoundland Regiment soldiers, heroes of the Somme, Arras, Cambrai and Gallipoli, all bearing marks of the Hun's savagery, arrived in this city yesterday on their

---

[1] G.W. Nicholson, The Fighting Newfoundlander.

way back to Blighty. Their presence at the Prince George Hotel was made known to the Red Cross and arrangements were hastily made to provide for their appearances in the huge pageant in Fifth Avenue today.

The story was from a journalist in the city of New York and appeared in the *Evening Telegram* on June 8, 1918. The ten soldiers included: Israel Bannister, captured and held as a POW; Sergeant Stewart Dewling, a medical corpsman who was given the Military Medal for removing the wounded while under fire – he accepted his medal while confined to a hospital bed by wounds received at the Somme; Second Lieutenant L.S. Field, nephew of Bishop Field; Captain Wilf Pippy; and Privates: L. Constantine, F.W. Dart, J.A. Moulton, L. Chaulk, L.M. Pennell, and S. Reid.

Israel Bannister did not receive a Victoria Cross, but his courage and battle successes during World War I brought him some attention in both New York and Newfoundland. He was singled out from among the ten because he was credited with killing over 500 German soldiers in defense of Monchy, during the Battle of Arras, in April 1917. In that battle he was taken prisoner after being wounded.

All ten soldiers were members of the Royal Newfoundland Regiment, 29th Division. The nine told the press how Bannister single-handedly held German troops back with his Lewis machine gun. They said he killed most of the attackers and put the others to rout. Only twelve Newfoundlanders survived the attack, out of a total of 300.

The story reported:

Like all their brother heroes: the Anzacs (Australians and New Zealanders), Blue Devils, and Canadians, who have reached this city in the last six months, these Newfoundlanders hesitate to tell of their individual heroism. They are full of praise for the 'other fellow', but make light of their own adventures in which they received wounds which have incapacitated them for life.

Among the group is Private Israel Bannister of the Royal Newfoundland Regiment of the Twenty-ninth Division, who is said to have slaughtered five hundred Germans with a machine gun in the defence of Monchy during the Battle of Arras in April 1917. He was severely wounded in action and taken prisoner.

After spending ten months in German prison camps, during which time he was subjected to all manner of brutality, he was traded with other wounded prisoners last Christmas and reached France by way of Switzerland.

After listening to Bannister's friends tell his story of courage under heavy fire, Bannister was asked to provide more details. He said:

They got me by a flanking movement of three divisions. I was in a shell hole and they tried to rout me out with artillery fire, but all the shots fell short. I saw where their battery was located, about sixteen hundred yards distant, so I ranged my gun and let fire. I think I got everyone in the battery because the gun went out of action. Then they got busy with the whiz bangs and shrapnel, which put me out of business. I was taken by (German) stretcher-bearers to a dressing station where after five hours they treated my wounds which were dressed with paper bandages. After that, they took me to a base hospital. The bandage was not changed for fourteen days.

Bannister spent ten months in a German prisoner-of-war camp where he was treated brutally. Describing conditions in the prison camp, Bannister said, "Without food from the Red Cross, prisoners would starve. We were given soup twice a day. It was just plain hot water with a few pieces of ordinary lawn grass, flavored with salt." Bannister made two unsuccessful escape attempts. For punishment he was confined to a small steam room, ten feet below ground, for ten days without food. There were six others in the room; three of them died. During Christmas 1917 Bannister was set free by the Germans as part of a prisoner exchange.

Sarah Holden Awarded Top Lady's Hero Award

Sarah Holden was born in St. John's in 1875 and during World War I served with the Red Cross and later the Royal Canadian

Army Medical Corps. She became a hero of the war after staying behind enemy lines with thirty-six injured soldiers until medical support arrived.

Sarah was educated in St. John's and earned a nursing degree at the Long Island School of Nursing, Brooklyn, New York. Upon graduation in 1909, she started her career as a night matron at the Long Island College Hospital.

When war broke out, she volunteered to work with the American Red Cross (ARC) in Europe. She was one of the first eleven nurses selected to go overseas with the ARC. The politics of war forced an end to Sarah's role in Europe. When it was learned that Sarah was a British subject, and with the United States being neutral, she was forced to resign from the ARC.

Sarah moved to Montreal where she joined the Royal Canadian Army Medical Corps in order to get back to the battlefront work. In mid-1915 Sarah was back in Europe with the rank of Lt. Nursing Sister. Her first assignment, which lasted a few months, was at an English military hospital. From there she was sent to the battlefront in Salonika, Greece. Tents served as hospital wards and there were heavy casualties. Although many nurses broke under the pressure, Sarah remained strong. On an occasion when the fighting line advanced, she was left behind as the only medical officer to care for thirty-six wounded men.

A bombing attack destroyed access roads and cut off the medical station from reinforcements for three days. When the reinforcements arrived, they found the patients in excellent condition and Nurse Holden still on her feet attending to her duties.

For her bravery and dedication, she earned the Royal Red Cross, one of the highest honours to be awarded to any woman during the war up to that time. Following the war, she returned to her nursing career in Brooklyn. She retired and moved to Montreal in 1953 where she passed away on February 4, 1960.

Heroine of War and the Spanish Flu

During 1918, the last year of the war, the Spanish Flu was sweeping the world. Throughout Europe and North America, an estimated 20 million people died from the disease. According to medical authorities, the spread of the flu in Newfoundland was checked by the cold winter.

On October 1, 1918, newspapers flashed the front page headline "Spanish Flu Strikes Town." Hundreds of cases were reported, mostly among foreign seamen in port. Public places were closed and a ban placed on all public gatherings. Due to overcrowding in city hospitals resulting from the epidemic, the King George V Institute on Water Street in St. John's was taken over and used as a hospital.

Ethel Dickinson, a niece of prominent city merchant James Pitts, was among the first to volunteer to work at the Institute. Ethel, who had served three years in France and Flanders nursing sick and wounded soldiers, was educated at the Methodist College, St. John's, and earned a teaching certificate in Chicago.

Within two weeks of working with the flu victims, Ethel contracted the disease and passed away. She had gotten the flu while accompanying patients to the emergency hospital in the old horse-drawn ambulance. She had left her protective face mask behind when she went out on a case. She was thirty-nine years old. Ethel was the only member of the medical profession in Newfoundland to die from the Spanish Flu. Because of the high risk involved in her volunteer work and the tremendous dedication shown by Ethel Dickinson, in the war and at home, she became an instant Newfoundland heroine.[2]

Health regulations then required victims of the epidemic to be buried immediately. Ethel Dickinson was buried that same afternoon. Two weeks later the epidemic had passed and the ban on public gatherings was lifted.

On October 27, 1920, the people of St. John's showed their recognition and appreciation of the unselfish spirit of Ethel Dickinson by unveiling the monument in her memory at Cavendish Square. Over time the Square was restructured and the monument moved to its present location on the island at Cavendish Square. It is fourteen feet high and made of Aberdeen granite surmounted by a Celtic Cross. It was unveiled by Governor Alexander Harris.

Cyril Gardner Captured Seventy-two Germans

Lt. Cyril Gardner of British Harbour, Trinity Bay, was at the centre of one of the most remarkable stories of WWI. In

---

[2] Jack Fitzgerald, <u>Strange But True Newfoundland Stories</u>.

recognition of his personal honour and courage, he was given the German Iron Cross by a German prisoner of war. This was a unique event because it was the enemy's top honour and it was presented to Gardner in the presence of a German platoon. Gardner was certainly not a traitor. However, he did perform an act of honour which the Germans considered to be noble and courageous.

Whether it was a coincidence or not, this amazing incident of war took place on January 27, 1917, the Kaiser's birthday. The allies planned a massive bombardment of German trenches, using five divisions, to deceive them into thinking a major offensive was underway. Gardner was among the company of Newfoundlanders held back in reserve.

The plan started at 5:30 a.m., and trench after trench held by the Germans was taken. The enemy had been taken completely by surprise. The Newfoundland Battalion started with a ten minute barrage of mortar fire from its trenches. Some Newfoundlanders being held in reserve, and watching the massive battle moving forward, decided to go into the battlefield as spectators. One of these was Cyril Gardner, then a Sgt. Major, who went into the danger without his gun. He reasoned that if questioned by senior officers he would say that he was out there keeping an eye on his men, some of whom were picking up the wounded.

Gardner was astounded to find that an enemy trench which he had thought to be vacated was occupied by German soldiers, heads down and obviously hoping not to be noticed by the troops advancing along the smoke-covered field. For a brief moment he must have regretted not taking his gun with him. Despite the fact that the Germans still had their weapons, Gardner took advantage of the smoke and confusion on the battlefield and, fearlessly and confidently, shouted into the trench, using words he hoped they would understand, "Tres bon. You're late. Everybody else has kameraded."

A soldier instantly dropped his gun and raised his hands into the air. Gardner took the opportunity to seize the discarded gun and, pointing it at the others, repeated his order. The Germans, who may not have understood his words, understood his gestures and the entire unit of seventy-two men surrendered.

While marching the prisoners back to his battalion, he was stopped by an English officer. After hearing what had happened, he congratulated Gardner, then began preparing his own gun for firing. He told Gardner that he intended to shoot the prisoners right there on the spot. Tension and fear spread among the Germans as they watched the aggressive actions of the officer.

Realizing the officer's intention, the Germans stepped backwards. At this point, Sgt. Gardner stepped in between the officer and the German soldiers and said, "Put your gun back, or for the first German that falls I'll shoot you." The officer hesitated, then put his gun away and retreated.

The German's senior officer, who wore many medals for bravery, stepped forward. He saluted Gardner and removing the Iron Cross from his own uniform, pinned it on Gardner's chest. All members of the German platoon applauded.

Military historian G. W. Nicholson described the incident. He said:

> Not often in the history of war has a soldier, in recognition of the heroic performance of his duty, received, at the hands of a foe, the highest military decoration which that enemy's army could bestow. By his own country, Gardner was awarded a *Bar to the Distinguished Conduct Medal* which he had won at Gueudecourt.

Soon after the first unsuccessful German counterattack, Gardner was given permission to go back to his vacated trench to recover his company's ration of rum for the day. It was a risky undertaken, but Gardner was a bold and fearless soldier who appreciated the value of the daily ration of rum to his fellow fighting men. He dodged German bullets, as his fellow soldiers watched and anxiously prayed for his safe return on this errand of mercy. Gardner disappeared into the smoke of the battlefield, and it was awhile before the figure of a soldier was seen emerging carrying a gallon jar. The cheers that greeted Gardner's safe return turned to groans when they saw how little was left in the jar.

The culprit who diminished the content of the jar was not Gardner. In tracking down the rum, he had discovered that another unit had moved into the trench and helped themselves to the rum. When Gardner entered the trench, the jar was being passed around with each soldier taking a nip. He had to pull rank on the men in order to recover the jar and its remaining contents.

In an earlier heroic incident, Gardner captured several German prisoners including two officers and forced the others to run from the battle. This action, for which he was awarded the Distinguished Conduct Medal, occurred on October 12, 1916. Gardner, from his trench, witnessed a German bombing party withdrawing from a failed assault on a nearby part of the Newfoundland Regiment's line. He led two soldiers in an attack on the German unit which caught them by surprise. Some Germans were shot and killed in the exchange that took place.

Gardner was promoted to 2nd Lieutenant but was killed in action at Monchy on April 14, 1917. Three hundred and sixty-eight Germans were taken prison on the Kaiser's birthday, June 27 1917, and Cyril Gardner was credited with the capture of seventy two of them.

Private J. B. Croak, Victoria Cross Winner

The first Newfoundlander to win a Victoria Cross was Private John Bernard Croak of Little Bay Mines.[3] Croak earned the coveted Victoria Cross while serving with the 13th Battalion Royal Highlanders of Canada during the Battle of Amiens, France. On August 9, 1918, the 13th Battalion launched a surprise attack on the German stronghold at Amiens. The battalion was led into battle by pipers with one of them playing from the top of an advancing tank.

In the midst of a raging battle, Croak became separated from his unit. While seeking his way through the blinding smoke of gun and shellfire, Croak stumbled upon a German machine gun nest. Single-handedly, using grenades and a machine gun, he attacked and silenced the enemy gunfire. The gun crew surrendered and was escorted by Croak back to his unit.

With the battle continuing, Croak returned to the frontlines and was seriously wounded. However, the injury did not deter him from fighting. When the gunfire slowed down, Croak used the opportunity to move towards enemy guns, firing as he attacked. His display of courage inspired others, and the remainder of his platoon followed him in a brilliant charge.

---

[3] The only member of the Newfoundland Regiment to be awarded a Victoria Cross was Thomas Ricketts, however, three other Newfoundlanders, serving with Canadian or British military were also awarded Victoria Crosses.

Croak led his comrades in capturing an entire German garrison. Later that day, Croak passed away from wounds received in battle. The citation for his Victoria Cross read, "The perseverance and valour of this gallant soldier who was severely wounded and died of his wounds were an inspiring example to all."

Croak was buried with his comrades near the spot where he fell in Amiens, France.

Newfoundland's "Ace" Naval Combatant

George Henry Rideout of Pilley's Island, Notre Dame Bay, penetrated enemy lines, knocked out a German communication's centre, and killed or wounded several German soldiers with no other weapon but an axe.

Rideouts outstanding display of courage occurred during August 1917 on a battlefield near the town of Ansoner in Serbia. Three thousand British forces were pinned down by German-Austrian forces in an almost continuous barrage of gunfire. The enemy and British forces were entrenched almost two miles apart. The open ground between them was filled with shell-torn pits and craters from the on-going battle.

Rideout, a member of the Royal Navy Reserve, was one of 3000 British soldiers pinned down near Ansoner. On the day of his heroic act, the Germans had maintained an endless bombardment of British trenches, and men were dying by the hundreds.

In order to understand the situation the British found themselves in that day, it is necessary to describe the battlefield positioning of the troops. On the left flank of the Germans, which was to the right of the battlefield, and slightly towards the front, was an enemy observation point. The Germans stationed in this position were able to determine the British range, and telephone the information to their gunners. This information enabled the Germans to drop shells directly in and around British trenches.

Unless something was done to knock out the observation post, the British forces faced being wiped out. The British quickly gathered intelligence showing that the wires of the telephone at the observation post ran from a tower through a communication's trench to the German batteries, and the British distance from these batteries was easily measured and acted upon.

Between 12:00 and 12:30 that night, the intensity of enemy fire had increased, and British soldiers were falling all around. It was at this point that Rideout and two others volunteered to go forward over the parapet, cross the shell-torn ground, and right up to the communication centre to knock out German communications.

In describing Rideout's mission a year later, the *Evening Telegram* reported, "To think of this was not the noble part. It was the voluntary offering to carry it out that was noble." The British Command agreed to the plan, and Rideout with his two companions set out on their daring mission with nothing but an axe each for a weapon.

The Germans had anticipated that the enemy would try to destroy their communication's operation. To protect it, they had stationed snipers at intervals along the telephone lines. The three volunteers slipped quietly over the top and into no-man's-land. Slowly, through hails of gunfire, they made their way towards the German lines. Machine gun and rifle fire were so relentless and deadly that the trio had to drop flat on their stomachs and crawl to the first available shell-hole.

The short consistent flashes of light, caused by exploding shells and bombs, provided sufficient brightness for the trio to keep moving towards their target. In leaps and bounds from one shell hole to another, they made their advances. All the way, they dodged bullets and the scanning eyes of the snipers.

Just before reaching their target, a bullet struck one of the volunteers and killed him instantly. The remaining two were not deterred. They bravely moved forward until they found themselves in a pit just in time to avoid detection by a passing German sentry. They remained pinned down by the constant gunfire for more than an hour.

Rideout made his move during a short interruption in gunfire. He moved quickly over the remaining few yards to the German communication lines, and with a few well placed slashes with his axe, he severed the wires and silenced the batteries.

By this time, a German sentry had seen Rideout's shadow moving over a clay background. The sentry rushed towards him with rifle and fixed bayonet and challenged him. On July 18, 1919, the *Evening Telegram* described the fight that ensued:

> With a side jump, Rideout avoids him – with an upward, and side slash of his axe, the German is stretched to the ground–dead. But the noise has brought another

German, and then another. Again, the axe is brought into play– again a German pays the penalty.

When Rideout was later asked how many of the enemy he had killed, he answered, "I didn't have time to count." Getting back to the British trenches was just as treacherous as the advance to the German line. A bullet, accidentally directed from the British side, struck and killed Rideout's partner.

Near the home-trenches, a British sentry challenged Rideout, who responded, "Britisher, I'm Rideout." The Newfoundlander was quickly surrounded and cheered by his fellow soldiers. The six-hour mission had ended in success, and although two of the three volunteers had lost their lives, hundreds of lives were saved by their bravery. Rideout, for his actions, was awarded the Victoria Cross (V.C.).

He gained the reputation of being 'Newfoundland's Ace' because of the awards he had earned. In addition to the V.C., he was awarded:

(1) The Egyptian Star which was presented by the Khedive of Egypt for service as a gunner on H.M.S. *Arphis* in capturing the towns of Gaza, Jaffa and Beirut.

(2) A medal for bravery which he earned in Gallipoli. Rear Admiral G. Jackson added a bar to this medal.

(3) The Royal Serbian Silver Medal; that was presented to him at Belgrade by the Crown Prince of Serbia, personally.

(4) He was also awarded the British Star and the Romanian Medal of Bravery.

Tommy Ricketts

Thomas "Tommy" Ricketts enlisted in the Newfoundland Regiment on September 2, 1916. This was same Thomas Ricketts who lied about his age to get into the Regiment at the height of World War I. On January 19, 1919, at Sandringham Palace Tommy would receive the Victoria Cross for courage and heroism from His Majesty, the King of England.

The event attracted many members of Royalty including: Prince Olaf of Norway, Queen Mary, Queen Alexandra, Queen Maud of Norway and Princess Victoria. There was a great deal of interest in the investiture of Ricketts with the V.C. because of his age. "Tommy," as his friends called him, was just eighteen years old and became the youngest person ever to receive the award. The oldest person awarded the Victoria Cross at the time was sixty-three year old Sir Dighton Probyn, who was among the guests at the palace to congratulate the young Newfoundlander. When the King presented Ricketts with the Victoria Cross, he noted that out of 7 million soldiers only 500 had earned the distinction of being awarded the Victoria Cross.

Thomas Ricketts, awarded the Victoria Cross. (Jack Fitzgerald)

Tommy Ricketts amazing act of heroism took place on October 14, 1918 near Ledgeham, Belgium. Three divisions of the German Axis troops were advancing in an attempt to capture part of a railroad which held great strategic importance. The 1st Battalion of the Royal Newfoundland Regiment was advancing with the 9th Division.[4]

Allied forces moved forward over a ridge through barbed wire entanglements, crossed a field sown with beet, and were stopped at a shallow ditch by a heavy barrage of German gunfire. German soldiers were barricaded inside two nearby farm houses with field guns and machine guns. The ditch afforded little protection for the allied forces, and the Germans shot down many of them.

The troops could neither advance nor retreat because the enemy had a complete sweep of the field with their artillery. Ricketts volunteered to go forward with Lance-Corporal Matthew Brazil of "B" Company, at great personal risk, to try and capture the enemy battery. They moved forward in short bursts to the extreme right of the enemy in an attempt to outflank them. The two soldiers succeeded in getting to about 300 yards when they ran out of ammunition. When the Germans realized that an effort was being made to clear their attacking wave, they took steps to move their guns back to a safer position. Ricketts anticipated the German move, and he took it upon himself to go back through

---

[4] By this stage of the war, the Newfoundland Regiment had been moved from the 29th Division to the 9th Division.

The farm outside Drie Masten, Belgium, where Private Tommy Ricketts earned his Victoria Cross in 1918. (PANL)

the hail of gunfire to get more ammunition. After collecting the ammunition, Ricketts dodged bullets all the way back to where he had left Brazil protecting the Lewis Gun.

The young Newfoundlander loaded the gun then went on the offensive against the German position. His use of the gun was so effective that the Germans retreated and took refuge in an abandoned farm where they were subsequently captured. This brave act of Ricketts enabled the platoon under Lieutenant Stan Newman to move in on the Germans without suffering any casualties. They took eight German prisoners, four field guns and four machine guns. When a fifth enemy field gun started to fire on them, they easily captured that as well.

Newfoundland's young hero had a private conversation with His Majesty, the King, during the presentation of the Victoria Cross at Sandringham Palace. King Geroge asked Ricketts if he remembered the visit of the HMS *Ophir* to Newfoundland at the beginning of the century. Ricketts answered that he did not. His Majesty then related several anecdotes about his reception in Newfoundland. In particular, his recollection of a handsome set of antlers he had viewed in the window of a Water Street store. "I was greatly taken with that head," said the King, "and I have often tried to remember the address of the place where I saw it, as I was always anxious to secure it."

The King and Queen along with their daughter Princess Victoria took Ricketts on a tour through the grounds of Sandringham. Not only was Thomas Ricketts honored by Britain, he was also recognized by the Government of France which awarded him the French Croix de Guerre.[5]

Part of his citation reads, "By his presence of mind in anticipating the enemy's intention and his utter disregard of personal safety, Ricketts secured a further supply of ammunition which directly resulted in these important captures and undoubtedly saved many lives.

When Tommy Ricketts returned home to Newfoundland he was given one of the greatest welcomes ever given to a Newfoundland hero. The Great War Veterans Association of Newfoundland through public subscription set up an annuity fund for him.

Tommy Ricketts operated a drug store at the corner of Job Street and Water Street for many decades. Well known St. John's pharmacist, Brian Healy, apprenticed with the famous war-hero at the Ricketts' drugstore on the western corner of Job Street and Water Street in the early 1960s.

Decorated by French

Albert Mugford of St. Carol's, French Shore, Newfoundland, was decorated by the French Government in 1917 for his gallantry in rescuing, single-handedly, the crew of a disabled French seaplane in the teeth of a raging gale and mountainous seas. He was given a hero's welcome when he arrived in St. John's from overseas duty in 1917.

At the time of earning the medal, Mugford, a Royal Naval Reservist, was attached to a patrol ship off the coast of France. While pounding their way through a swift running sea, the usual life of a patrol boat, they sighted a sea plane in distress and bearing down upon her, a boat was launched to rescue the crew who were clinging to the doomed craft.

Mugford was one of four men assigned for the rescue. After pulling away from the ship's side, it was discovered that the boat

---

[5] Captain L.C. Murphy, <u>The Newfoundland Magazine</u>, April 1919. Murphy was a witness to Rickett's heroism.

was too small to take on the stranded crew. The rescue crew were forced to return to their ship. While the captain pondered the next move, Mugford lowered himself into the boat, and volunteered to go to the rescue alone. Permission was granted.

He fought the violent waves and removed the men one-by-one from the disabled machine. After rescuing the crew, he went back to attempt to tow the seaplane, but just as he got near, it was swallowed by the sea. Meanwhile, the storm had worsened. The winds became stronger and the waves higher. Mugford had to battle his way back to his ship. He succeeded, and, when he climbed back on board, was given a hero's welcome.

The *Daily News* on December 30, 1918, refers to a Private Mugford, born in Newfoundland, serving with Canadian forces, and being awarded a Victoria Cross.

Private John Fitzgerald Hero off Gallipoli

Private John Fitzgerald of Queen's Road, St. John's, Newfoundland, served with the Royal Newfoundland Regiment's Medical section at Gallipoli in 1915. On December 1st, in the aftermath of The Great Storm, he lost his life in an act of heroism. For this he was recommended for the Victoria Cross and listed in the regiment's "Honours and Awards List" under the category "Mentioned in Dispatches."

On the morning of that day, Quartermaster, Sergeant Norman Mcleod, and Lance Corporal Hubert Ebsary were forced to walk in an open ground area due to the trenches having been flooded and washed away. At about 150 yards from the Newfoundland lines, a sniper's bullet hit Ebsary. McLeod immediately went to his aid.

Fitzgerald witnessed the action and rushed back from the front lines accompanied by a stretcher bearer who was killed by a sniper's bullet when they reached the wounded soldier. Another shot rang out which struck McLeod. Fitzgerald left Ebsary so he could dress McLeod's wound. While returning to aid Ebsary, a sniper's bullet hit Fitzgerald in the leg. Despite his wound, the medic continued to giving medical assistance.

He worked away, ignoring the sounds of gunfire and the dangers around him. Later McLeod reported that he heard Fitzgerald say, "Mac, I'm hit again," but he persisted until a third bullet hit him. At this time, he groaned then fell beside Ebsary. When help arrived, both Ebsary and Fitzgerald were dead.

Private F. T. Lind who was on the battlefield at the time later said:

> Jack (John) Fitzgerald was one of the bravest in the whole war. The morning the others were shot, he took his Red Cross satchel and went out in the midst of the hail of bullets and began to bandage the wounds. One bullet struck him, and he staggered for a moment, then went on with his work of binding the wounds of his comrade, but shortly after, he fell and when we brought his body in, there were five bullets in him.[6]

Lind said that the whole Regiment mourned Fitzgerald's loss. Private Fitzgerald did not get a Victoria Cross, however, his mother erected an appropriate monument on the family grave at Belvedere Cemetery in his memory. According to Lind, Fitzgerald was actually buried at Azmak Cemetery, Gallipoli.[7]

In 2008, vandals destroyed the monument at Belvedere Cemetery, leaving it broken and in several pieces.

A Hero at Gallipoli

Private William Gladney was awarded the Distinguished Conduct Medal for his performance at Gallipoli. At a point in battle, when the Turks had the Newfoundland Regiment pinned down with heavy fire from concealed weapons, Gladney volunteered to take them out. On his own, he ventured from friendly trenches out into no-man's-land, crawling on his hands and knees in a mission that seemed impossible.

In a position directly in front of the enemy trenches were two guards in dugouts who were rotated with replacements hourly. When Gladney got close to the dugouts, which were twenty-five yards from the guns, he succeeded in taking out the two guards. He then took over the dugout which gave him a close up view of the four machine guns. Gladney took time to draw a rough sketch of the position of each attacking gun. Once completed, he crawled back to his own trenches and passed his sketches over to senior officers.

---

[6] Dr. David Facey-Crowther, <u>Better Than the Best</u>.
[7] G.W. Nicholson, <u>The Fighting Newfoundlander</u>, p184.

This photo shows the plaque presented to the parents of Private David Carew, who was shot by a sniper at Gallipoli in 1915. The photo displays the Union Jack on the left, and the Newfoundland flag on the right. This was the flag under which Newfoundlanders fought and died in WWI. King George V is shown between the two flags. These plaques were issued to all families who lost a son, or sons in WWI. It reads: The Great European War 1914. (Courtesy of Owen and Jean (Carew) Moore)

Private Gladney attempted to return to the enemy dugouts accompanied by an officer, but by that time, the Turks, allies of the Germans, had been alerted. The two soldiers abandoned the mission. Gladney's information enabled the Regiment to break the battlefield deadlock. Soon after, he was promoted from Private to Sergeant. Gladney was among those wounded at Gallipoli and, along with other heroes of that campaign, returned home. The soldiers arrived by railway express in St. John's on August 7, 1916. Thousands turned out to give them a hero's welcome at the railway station.

Gladney, although born in Canada, moved to Portugal Cove at a young age where he lived with his aunt, Bridget Gladney. He was educated at St. Bonaventure's College and enlisted in the Newfoundland Regiment at the start of the war.

Over thirty-five percent of the 1000 residents of the community of Portugal Cove, located not far from St. John's, answered "The call of Empire."[8]

Victoria Cross

Most people believe that the Victoria Cross takes precedence over all other orders and decorations in the British Empire. However, there is no evidence to support this belief. The Encyclopedia of Newfoundland, edited by J.R. Smallwood, points out that, "nowhere in any Royal Warrant has reference been found to establish such precedence". The award was instituted in 1856 by Queen Victoria to be awarded to, "... those officers or men who served us in the presence of the enemy and shall have performed some single act of valour or devotion to their country."

Only 1347 people have received the prestigious award since 1856; four of them were Newfoundlanders. Thomas Ricketts was the only one serving with the Newfoundland Regiment. The others served with the Royal Navy or Canadian forces.

The Battle Before the Battle!

Prior to the Battle of Beaumont Hamel, the Newfoundland Regiment made a raid on the German Front lines to prepare for the major battle about to be launched. In preparation, the General in charge called together the entire division to describe

---

[8] The Evening Telegram, August 7, 1916, p7.

the great assault that was approaching. He discussed the issues that depended upon their success as well as the odds in favour of victory. The soldiers were in high spirits by the time the General finished.

In the days before the battle, sixty members of the New-foundland Regiment, led by two officers, carried out two raids upon the German front lines. In the first raid, they succeeded in cutting pathways through several portions of the barbed wire fence erected by the Germans. When they returned the next night, they saw that the Germans had detected the cut wires and were waiting for them. The Germans had fixed machine guns covering the openings in the barbed wire.

The Newfoundlanders cautiously moved towards the enemy guns. The *Evening Telegram* on July 28, 1916, reported that before the machine guns could get into action, the Newfoundlanders were sweeping down upon the German gunners with bombs. It said:

> Others leaped into the German trench and some stationed themselves so as to cover the entrance to the dug-out, killing the Germans as they emerged. At one point a machine gun threatened to do some damage, but into that corner went a private named George Phillips with a bayonet.

> Phillips was pinned down in the trench until early next morning when he made his way back to camp with his warning that the enemy was waiting at the openings with many machine guns.

Thoughts of a Hero

The *London Daily News* on July 8, 1916, quoted a survivor's description of what he thought and felt as he went towards the constant barrage of fire from the enemy lines at Beaumont Hamel. The article was titled, *The Dash of the Newfoundlanders-No Thoughts But to get Through*. It reported:

> There were innumerable German machine guns, and these began to sweep across the land like a driving rain on a Scotch more. Men began to drop, but the rest moved on like steady veterans.

'I was curiously void of any feeling except a determination to get through,' said one who was in the charge, ' and I believe all the boys were the same. The roar of the British artillery seemed but a murmur in that rush and though the German bullets were sweeping the tops of the grass so completely as to give an impression of a heavy wind, nobody seemed to care. I now recall that in civil life when I saw an accident I felt the horror of it, but in that attack I thought no more of falling men than of flicking the ash off a cigarette. How does it feel to be in a charge? It feels like nothing at all– you just go forward.'

Appendix to Chapter 7

Honours Awarded to Royal Newfoundland Regiment Members

The following is a list of those in the Royal Newfoundland Regiment who were decorated during WWI. It is in the order of precedence recommended in 1965 by the Director of Army Personnel in Ottawa.

The Engagement Column is used with the following decorations: Victoria Cross, Distinguished Service Order, Bar to Distinguished Service Order; Distinguished Conduct Medal, Bar to Distinguished Conduct Medal; Military Medal, Bar to Military Medal.

While in most cases "Mentioned in Despatches" and "Foreign Decorations" were also awarded for service at the front, they were usually given as an additional honour and rarely accompanied by a special citation, and for these reasons the 'Engagement Column ' has been left blank in connection with these two categories.

The word "Periodic", used on a few instances under 'Engagement,' is applied where the award was not given for any particular engagement, but for continuous devotion to duty and gallant conduct throughout.

The rank shown in each instance is the highest rank obtained by a recipient as far as can be determined and in many cases will not correspond to that held at the time of the award.

Those, from other units, who were awarded honours and decorations while serving with the Royal Newfoundland Regiment, such as Colonel W. H. Franklin and Lt.-Col. F. Robertson, have an asterisk after their name when it first appears in the list.[9]

An asterisk is also used in for men who served temporarily with an auxiliary or supplementary unit of the Newfoundland Regiment such as the "Machine Gun Corps."

---

[9] PANL MG 438.

REG. #	RANK	NAME	ENGAGEMENT
		Victoria Cross	
3102	Sgt.	Ricketts, Thomas	
		Companion of the Order of St. Michael and St. George	
	Lt.-Col.	Hadow, Arthur L., C.M.G.	
	Lt.-Col.	Macpherson, Cluny, C.M.G.	
		Commander of the Order of the British Empire	
	Col.	Franklin, W. H., C.B.E., O.B.E.*	
	Lt.-Col.	Montgomerie, Alexander, C.B.E., O.B.E.	
	Col.	Rendell, Walter F., C.B.E.	
		Distinguished Service Order	
146	Major	Butler, Bertram, D.S.O., M.C. & Bar Cambrai	
	Lt.-Col.	Forbes-Robertson, James, V.C., D.S.O., M.C.*Monchy-le-Preux	
	Lt.-Col.	Woodruffe, J.S., D.S.O. Armentieres	
		Office of the Order of the British Empire	
1879	Capt.	Emerson, George M., O.B.E.	
	Major	Greene, W. H., O.B.E.	
	Major	Knight, J. St. P., O.B.E.	
	Capt.	McNeill, Hector, O.B.E.	
	Lt.-Col.	Montgomerie, Alexander, C.B.E., O.B.E.	
	Lt.-Col.	Paterson, Lamont, O.B.E.	
	Lt.-Col.	Timewell, H. A., O.B.E.	
894	Capt.	Whitty, Gerald J., O.B.E., M.C.	
		Member of the Order of the British Empire	
	Capt.	Anderson, H.A., M.B.E.	
872	Capt.	Duley, Cyril C., M.B.E.	
	Major	Howley, J.M., M.B.E.	
608	Major	Marshall, Fred W., M.B.E.	
	Capt.	O'Grady, J.J. M.B.E.	
	Capt.	Outerbridge, Herbert A., M.B.E.	
	Lieut.	Rees, William, M.B.E.	
	Capt.	Rennie, William H., M.B.E.	
	Lieut.	Winter, Herbert M., M.B.E.	
		Royal Victoria Order	
1862	Bandmaster	Worthington, Lewis Llewelyn, R.V.O.	
		Military Cross	
166	Capt.	Bartlett, Rupert W., M.C. & Bar Les Fosses Farm	
	Lt.-Col.	Bernard, A.E., M.C.	Periodic
146	Major	Butler, Bertram, D.S.O., M.C. & Bar	Beaumont Hamel
340	Captain	Byrne, Gerald G., M.C.	Sailly-Saillisel
52	Capt.	Chafe, Eric R. A., M.C.	Broombeek
503	Capt.	Clift, John, M.C.	Armentieres
	Capt.	Donnelly, James J., M.C.	Caribou Hill
	Lt.-Col.	Forbes-Robertson, James, V.C., D.S.O., M.C.	Periodic
58	Capt.	Frost, C. Sydney, M.C.	Keilberg Ridge
334	Lieut.	Goodyear, Stanley C., M.C.	Periodic
833	Capt.	Hicks, H. George, M.C. & Bar	Broombeek
2915	Lieut.	Hopson, Frank H., M.C.	Ledgehem
766	Capt.	Keegan, Kevin J., M.C. & Bar	Monchy-le-Preux
	Major	March, J. Wesley, M.C.	Gueudecourt
419	Lieut.	Mifflin, James, M.C.	Cambrai
36	Capt.	Newman, Albert Stanley, M.C.	Ledeghem
	Capt.	Nunns, Joseph, M.C.	Broembeek
594	Capt.	Paterson, R. Grant, M.C. & Bar	Steenbeek
1741	Lieut.	Postlethwaite, Robert A., M.	Periodic
	Major	Raley, Arthur, M.C.	Periodic
	Capt.	Rendell, Herbert, M.C.	Cambrai
	Capt.	Rowsell, Reginald S., M.C.	Periodic
46	Capt.	Stick, J. Robin, M.C.	Periodic
	Major	Tait, Robert H. M.C.	Broombeek
1554	2nd.Lt.	Taylor, Albert E., M.C. & Bat, D.C.M. *	Broombeek
	Capt.	Toucher, J.W., M.C.	Monchy-le-Preux
441	Lieut.	Waterman, Frederick W., M.C.	Periodic
894	Capt.	Whitty, Gerald J., O.B.E., M.C.	Cambrai
1759	Lieut.	Williamson, Harry, M.C.	Keiberg Ridge

	Major	Windeler, Henry S., M.C. *	Bellenglise

*While temporarily attached to 46th Battalion, Machine Gun Corps.

166	Capt.	Bartlett, Rupert W. M.C. & Bar.	Steenbeek
146	Major	Butler, Bertram, D.S.O., M.C. & Bar	Guedecourt
833	Capt.	Hicks, H. George, M.C. & Bar	Ledeghem
766	Capt.	Keegan, Kevin J., M.C. & Bar	Broombeek
504	Capt.	Paterson, R. Grant,M.C. & Bar	Cambrai
1554	2nd Lieut.	Taylor, Alberte, M.C. & Bar	Keiberg Ridge

Distinguished Conduct Medal

2247	Pte.	Anthony, William, D.C.M.	Ledeghem
1071	L/Cpl.	Bennett, William, D.C.M.	Gueudecourt
1368	Cpl.	Brazil, Matthew, D.C.M., M.M.	Ledeghem
1403	Sgt.	Carter, Charles F., D.C.M.	Ledeghem
3423	Pte.	Corbin, Thomas, D.C.M.	Ledeghem
2057	2nd Lt.	Davis, Albert, D.C.M., M.M.	Cambrai
1438	2nd Lt.	Dunphy, Thomas J., D.C.M.	Steenbeek
793	Sgt.	Fitzpatrick, Leo J., D.C.M.	Cambrai
824	2nd Lt.	Gardner, Cyril, D.C.M. & Bar	Gueudecourt
417	Sgt.	Gladney, William J., D.C.M.	Gallipoli
266	2nd	Greene, Walter M., D.C.M.	Caribou Hill
3289	L/Cpl.	Greenslade, Samuel, D.C.M.	Ledeghem
1385	R.S.M.	Gullicksen, Ernest, D.C.M.	Armentieres
1974	2nd Lt.	Hynes, Richard E., D.C.M.	Armentieres
1539	Cpl.	Hollett, Levi, D.C.M.	Broembeek
807	L/Cpl.	Hynes, Richard E., D.C.M.	Caribou Hill
702	C.S.M.	Janes, Albert E., D.C.M.	Cambrai
2181	Sgt.	Murphy, James J. D.C.M.	Broombeek
3481	Pte.	O'Quinn, James H. , D.C.M.	Keiberg Ridge
2010	Sgt.	Picco, Martin, D.C.M.	Sailly-Saillisel
1733	Cpl.	Pittman, Thomas A., D.C.M. M.M.	Periodic
2603	Cpl.	Power, Richard, D.C.M.	Ledeghem
916	Sgt.	Purcell, Roderick, D.C.M.	Broembeek
801	Cpl.	Raynes, Harry R., D.C.M.	Steenbeek
1826	2nd Lt.	Rose, Albert S.D.C.M., M.M.	Ledeghem
267		C.S.M. Samson, Peter, D.C.M.	Gueudecourt
378	Sgt.	Spurrell, Charles P., D.C.M.	Broombeek
1308	2nd. Lt.	Stanford, Reginald F. D.C.M.	Keiberg Ridge
1726	Sgt.	Sutton, William, D.C.M.	Keiberg Ridge
1554	2nd. Lt.	Taylor, Albert E., M.C. & Bar, D.C.M.	Periodic
3382	Cpl.	Whalen, Arthur S., D.C.M.	Ledeghem

Bar to Distinguished Conduct Medal

824	2nd Lt	Gardner, Cyril, D.C.M. & Bar.	Lesboeufs

Military Medal

168	Pte.	Abbott, Jacob, M.M.	Broembeek
1989	Cpl.	Adams, Alexander, M.M. & Bar	Broembeek
643	Sgt.	Aitken, Ernest P., M.M. & Bar	Broembeek
798	2nd.Lt.	Barrett, Harold G. M.M.	Gueudecourt
3187	Pte.	Bendell, Freeman, M.M.	Armentiers
1785	Pte.	Bennett, Manuel, J., M.M.	Cambrai
42	Cpl.	Best, Frank Gordon, M.M.	Yser Canal
526	Pte.	Bowden, Hugh Pierson	Broembeek
1368	Cpl.	Brazil, Matthew, D.C.M., M.M.	Armentiers
1319	Pte.	Brown, David, M.M.	Gueudecourt
2427	L/Cpl.	Bulgin, Augustus, M.M.	Broembeek
3117	C.S.M.	Burge, Daniel, M..M.	Armentiers
430	A/C S.M.	Butcher, Ernest, M.M.	Broembeek
796	C.S.M.	Butler, Harold S., S.M.	Broembeek
1903	Cpl.	Carroll, Bernard, M.M.	Gueudecourt
1927	C.Q.M.S.	Cheeseman, E.B., M.M.	Cambrai
1455	L/Cpl.	Clark, Howard S., M.M.	Periodic
3642	Pte.	Clarke, John, M.M.	Ledeghem
863	Cpl.	Collins, John J., M.M.	Cambrai
710	Sgt.	Collins, Matthew, M.M.	Gueudecourt
1141	L/Cpl.	Cook, Thomas, M.M.	Cambrai
809	Sgt.	Cox, John, M.M.	Beaumont Hamel
1335	Sgt.	Curnew, Charles, M.M.	Armentiers
122	Pte.	Curran, D. Wilfred, M.M.	Monchy-le-Preux
1552	Pte.	Curtis, Doyle, M.M.	Ledeghem
2057	2nd.Lt.	Davis, Albert, D.C.M., M.M.	Cambrai

738	Pte.	Davis, John, M.M.	Broembeek
3011	Pte.	Dawe, Frank, M.M.	Steenbeek
20	C.S.M.	Dewling, Steward, M.M.	Beaumont Hamel
2935	Pte.	Dibben, Hubert, M.M.	Cambrai
2098	Cpl.	Dunn, James, M.M.	Broembeek
793	Sgt.	Fitzpatrick, Leo J., D.C.M., M.M.	Broembeek
1025	Pte.	Fowlow, William, M.M.	Cambrai
645	Sgt.	Gardner, Hamar, M.M.	Ledeghem
154	C.S.M.	Gooby, Archibald, M.M.	Monchy-le-Preux
1834	Pte.	Goodland, Oliver, M.M.	Gueudecourt
2473	Pte.	Gosse, John, M.M.	Armentieres
2511	Sgt.	Goudie, Ernest, M.M. & Bar	Broembeek
1918	Pte.	Gough, Newman, M.M.	Keiberg Ridge
2843	C.S.M.	Greene, Gregory L., M.M.	Keiberg Ridge
978	Cpl.	Hagen, James, G., M.M. & Bar	Cambrai
79	C.S.M.	Hammond, Arthur, M.M.	Steenbeek
461	Sgt.	Hennebury, Alexander, M.M.	Broembeek
3346	Pte.	Hennebury, John, M.M.	Cambrai
1878	S/Sgt.	Hillier, John H. M.M.	Monchy-le-Preux
2110	L/Cpl.	Hounsell, Japhet H., M.M.	Monchy-le-Preux
2536	Sgt.	Jewer, Walter, M.M.	Broembeek
502	Sgt.	Joy, Edward, M.M.& Bar	Cambrai
1376	Cpl.	Joy, William, M.M.	Ledeghem
2577	Pte.	King, William, M.M.	Ledeghem
2052	Pte.	Knee, Henry, M.M.	Cambrai
2344	Pte.	Lacey, George B., M.M.	Steenbeek
2094	2nd Lt.	Le Drew, Ralph, M.M.	Cambrai
3216	Pte.	Lee, Albert, M.M.	Keilberg Rdige
2144	Sgt.	Lewis, John P., M.M.	Sailly-Saillisel
163	Cpl.	Lidstone, Harold, M.M.	Yser Canal
2970	Pte.	Loveless, John, M.M.	Cambrai
230	Cpl.	McDonald, Patrick Q. M.M.	Broembeek
856	Pte.	McGrath, Thomas, M.M.	Beaumont Hamel
721	Cpl.	Manuel, Alfred, M.M.	Gueudecourt
1709	Pte.	Meaney, Thomas, M.M. & Bar	Steenbeek
885	C.Q.M.S.	Mews. Percival C., M.M.	Ledeghem
2262	Pte.	Mooney, John, E., M.M.	Ledeghem
825	Pte.	Moore, Leo, M.M.	Cambrai
2987	L/Cpl.	Moore, William, M.M.	Broembeek
689	Sgt.	Morrissey, John J., M.M.	Gueudecourt
2760	Pte.	Mullett, George, M.M. & Bar	Steenbeek
3582	Pte.	Murphy, A.John, M.M.	Keiberg Ridge
2108	Pte.	Murray, Arthur, M.M.	Steenbeek
1080	Sgt.	Neville, Richard, M.M.	Gueudecourt
129	L/Cpl.	Nichol, John E., M.M.	Broembeek
3603	Pte.	O'Brien, Edward, M.M.	Ledeghem
2263	Pte.	O'Neill, Patrick, M.M.	Steenbeek
3345	L/Cpl.	O'Rourke, John, M.M.	Keiberg Ridge
2558	Pte.	Paddick, Levi, M.M.	Broembeek
1604	Cpl.	Pafford, Chesley, M.M.	Broembeek
783	Sgt.	Parsons, Charles, M.M. & Bar	Monchy-le-Preux
705	Pte.	Peddle, John K., M.M.	Steenbeek
1164	Pte.	Phillips, George, M.M.	Beaumont Hamel
2115	Sgt.	Pitcher, Walter, M.M.	Monchy-le-Preux
1733	Cpl.	Pittman, Thomas A., D.C.M., M.M.	Cambrai
2318	C.S.M.	Power, Maurice, M.M.	Vichte
1281	Pte.	Power, Pierce, M.M.	Cambrai
2603	Cpl.	Power, Richard, D.C.M., M.M.	Ledeghem
2626	L/Cpl.	Rees, Frederick, S., M.M.	Broembeek
3120	Pte.	Reid, Bramwell B, M.M.	Broembeek
1826	2nd Lt.	Rose, Albert S., D.C.M., M.M.	Monchy-le-Preux
2079	L.Cpl.	Rose, John, M.M.	Steenbeek
958	Pte.	Saunders, W. Roy, M.M.	Armentieres
88	Pte.	Simms, John, M.M.	Steenbeek
1393	Sgt.	Smith, Andrew, M.M.	Ledeghem
685	L/Cpl.	Snow, Frederick E., M.M.	Gallipoli
3362	Sgt.	Snow, Harry, M.M.	Armentieres
2291	Pte.	Spurrell, Heber, M.M.	Steenbeek
1747	L/Cpl.	Stacey, Alfred J., M.M.	Cambrai
2145	Cpl.	Stick, E. Moyle., M.M.	Escaping Captivity
2786	Cpl.	Sullivan, Peter, M.M.	Armentieres
2040	Cpl.	Tansley, Harry, M.M.	Broembeek
3498	L/Cpl.	Thomas, H. Gordon, M.M.	Armentiers

3156	Pte.	Trask, Heber, M.M.	Ledeghem
1792	Cpl.	Walsh, Michael, M.M.	Ledeghem
789	Sgt.	Waterfield, Joseph R., M.M.	Monchy-le-Preux
236	Sgt.	Webber, Arthur, M.M.	Gueudecourt
3612	Cpl.	White, Samuel, M.M.	Armentieres
2896	Sgt.	Winter, Marmaduke G., M.M.	Cambrai
2523	Cpl.	Wiseman, Ebenezer G. M.M.	Steenbeek
3880	Sgt.	Woolfrey, Wilfred J., M.M.	Ledeghem
1700	L./Cpl.	Yetman, Nathan, M.M.	Armentieres

Bar to Military Medal

1989	Cpl.	Adams, Alexander, M.M.& Bar	Ledeghem
643	Sgt.	Atkins, Ernest, M.M. & Bar	Ledeghem
2511	Sgt.	Goudie, Ernest, M.M.&Bar	Cambrai
978	Cpl.	Hagen, James G.W., M.M.&Bar	Armentieres
502	Sgt.	Joy, Ed, M.M.& Bar	Cambrai
1709	Pte.	Meaney, Thomas J., M.M.&Bar	Broembeek
2760	Pte.	Mullett, George, M.M. & Bar	Keiberg Ridge
783	Sgt.	Parsons, Charles, M.M. & Bar.	Cambrai

Meritorious Service Medal

8230	Sgt.	Ball, A.F.	
6195	Sgt.	Bursell, Sydney, M.S.M.	
905	Sgt.	Butler, Charles, M.S.M.	
221	Sgt.	Canham, Arthur R., M.S.M.	
1529	S/Sgt.	Crocker, A.G., M.S.M.	
984	S/Sgt.	Green, Cecil, M.S.M.	
360	S/Sgt.	Hammond, Thomas, M.S.M.	
109	2nd Lt.	Janes, Harold C., M.S.M.	
387	S/S.M.	Lambert, James, M.S.M.	
8115	Sgt.	Lane, Enos, M.S.M.	(Newfoundland Forestry Corps)
535	S/Sgt.	Lawlor, Thomas J., M.S.M.	
1861	Capt.	McKay, J. M. , M.S.M.	
8209	Sgt.	Morey, Philip, M.S.M.	(Newfoundland Forestry Corps)
701	C.Q.M.S	Stephenson, David, M.S.M.	
2406	C.Q.M.S.	Watson, James, M.S.M.	
674	2nd Lt.	Wellman, Edward, M.S.M.	
171	2nd Lt.	White, Charles E., M.S.M.	

Mentioned in Dispatches

3182	C.S.M.	Anstey, Albert I..
575	Sgt.	Ash, Archibald
	Lt.-Col.	Bernard, A.E. M.C.
146	Major	Butler, Bertram, D.S.O., M.C. & Bar
966	Pte.	Cahill, John J.
536	2nd.Lt.	Clare, William Joseph
295	Pte.	Fitzgerald, John M.
		Forbes-Robertson, James, V.C. , D.S.O.., M.C
417	Sgt.	Gladney, William, J., D.C.M.
	Lt.-Col.	Hadow, Arthur L., C.M.G.
	Lieutenant	Holloway, R.P.
249	Lt.-Cpl.	Jesseau, Arthur F.
2285	Lieut.	McHenry, William E.
31	Capt.	McNeill, Hector, O.B.E.
	L./Col.	MacPherson, Cluny, C.M.G.
159	C.S.M.	Mercer, Fred
664	C.S.M.	Nicholle, Edward H.
	Capt.	O'Brien, Augustus
402	Pte.	O'Neill, Frederick M.
3920	C.S.M.	Parsons, John W.
	Capt.	Rendell, Herbert, M.C.
	Lieut.	Waterman, Frederick W., M.C.
2406	C.Q.M.S.	Watson, James, M.S.M.
	Lt.-Col	Whitaker, C.W. (Home Dispatches)
1759	Lieut.	Williamson, Harry, M.C.

		Honourable Mention to Secretary of State for War
	Capt.	Anderson, H.A., M.B.E.

	Lt. Col.	Carty, George T.
622	Lieut.	Clouston, Andrew M.
	Major	Greene, W.H., O.B.E.
	Capt.	Karn, J. Cyril
1861	Capt.	MacKay, J. Murdoch, M.S.M.
	Lt.-Col.	Macpherson, Cluny, C.M.G.
608	Major	Marshall, Fred, M.B.E.
	Col.	Rendell, Walter F., C.B.E.
		Lt.-Col. Whitaker, C.W.

Foreign Awards
French

		Croix de Guerre
	Lt.-Col.	Bernard, A.E., M.C.
	Major	March, J. Wesley, M.C.
801	Cpl.	Raynes, Harry R., D.C.M.
267	C.S.M.	Samson, Peter, D.C.M.

		Croix de Guerre avec Etoile d'Or
3102	Sgt.	Ricketts, Thomas, V.C.

		Croix de Guerre avec d'Argent
	Major	Raley, Arthur, M.C.

		Croix de Guerre avec Etoile de Bronze
3481	O'Quinn,	James H., D.C.M.
2603	Cpl.	Power, Richard, D.C.M., M.M.
1308	2nd. Lt .	Stanford, Reginald F., D.C.M.

		Medaille d' Honneur avec Glaives en Bronze
1385	R.S.M.	Gullicksen, Ernest, D.C.M.

Belgian

		Chevalier de L'Ordre de Leopold II
3849	Sgt.	Bishop, John E.

		Croix de Guerre
1438	2nd Lt.	Dunphy, Thomas J., D.C.M.
1385	R.S.M.	Guillicksen, Ernest, D.C.M.
1539	Cpl.	Hollett, Levi, D.C.M.
2285	Lieut.	McHenry, William E.
	Lt.-Col.	Mathias, D.G., D.S.O.*
1012	C.S.M.	Meadus, Allan George
1256	Sgt.	Somerton, Frank H.
1726	Sgt.	Sutton, William, D.C.M.

*Awarded the D.S.O. while serving with the Welch Regiment

Italian

166	Capt.	Bartlett, Rupert W., M.C. & * Bar
		Italian Bronze Medal
236	Sgt.	Webber, Arthur, M.M

Russian

		Medal of St. George
1164	Pte.	Phillips, George, M.M. . .

Chapter 8

THE LAST DAYS

An Air Base at Cape Race

In mid-June 1918, when there was concern that Germany might attack St. John's and concentrate on shipping along the Newfoundland coast, planning was in progress to establish a land and sea air base in Cape Race. The strategists, struggling with the problem of how to best deal economically with the German threat to St. John's and coastal area, proposed two choices. The first was the suggestion to install heavy guns at St. John's Harbour and have armed patrol boats operating from there and ready to respond. The second proposal was to provide air surveillance using aeroplanes and or seaplanes.

The Newfoundland Government followed up both ideas by obtaining the advice of an expert on coastal defence who, after studying the problem, recommended that Government proceed with the plan to use an air defence. It was pointed out that an air patrol was faster and cheaper than the alternative. The British Government wanted both heavy guns and air patrols, but it was too late in the summer to do anything about it.

The move to set up an air base did get underway with Canada taking the initial steps. Its plan was to construct a base at Cape Race which would handle land planes, seaplanes, airship balloons, and kite balloons, all were to be equipped with the latest suitable instruments.

Canada, Britain and the United States favoured the building of an air station in St. John's as an, "...outpost to the bigger station at Cape Race." Britain agreed to consult with its air force experts. The American Aviation Construction Department said it could supply aeroplane model J.N.4.H., which would be fitted with a Hispano/Suiza engine with bomb dropping ability, wireless and all the latest technology. Two planes were immediately ready for the new air base and two more shortly after. The cost of each aircraft was $8500. The idea for motor patrol boats was dropped because it would have been too costly.[1]

---

[1] PANL GN2 14.

The project ended with the ending of the war on November 11, 1918.

German Collapse

Leading up to the November 11th Armistice, there was extensive diplomatic activity going on, particularly between the Germans and President Woodrow Wilson. The Germans indicated they were willing to meet Allied demands that they immediately stop the inhumane practice of using poison gas, and they agreed to withdraw their troops into Germany. This led to the Armistice and the end to the war. In Germany, a new German Republic was proclaimed by the Social Democrats and some socialists. Its leader became Friedrich Ebert.

On October 26, 1918, the German Supreme Commander, General Eric Ludendorff, resigned and refused to participate in a surrender. This enabled Hitler to later claim that Germany had not lost the war on the battlefield but was betrayed by its politicians who "...stabbed Germany in the back."

In fact, it was the long drawn out drudgery and suffering caused by the war that resulted in the loss of the German Army's will to fight. In their book, *Marching to Armageddon*, Morton and Granatstein explained why it could be stated that Germany was not beaten:

> Her army had 2.5 million men. Her conquests were intact. Her most powerful enemies were exhausted, as Canadians and Australians had painfully discovered at Amiens. What was gone was von Ludendorff's will to fight. That, like Bolshevism, was a communicable disease.

On October 28th, the Kaiser was stripped of all duties and Germany was run by its Reichstag. The German Army refused to fight and its Navy, at Kiel, mutinied on November 3rd. They seized Kiel and raised the Communist red flag. This was followed by their setting up councils of workers and sailors. This mutiny spread to other cities.

Around this period, an event occurred which embarrassed the government of the United States. The US had launched a premature day of celebrations after being mistakenly informed by their diplomats of the wrong date for the signing of the armistice.

In victory, the Royal Newfoundland Regiment crossing the Rhine at the end of WW1. (PANL)

The armistice was signed on November 11, 1918, at 5:00 a.m. in a railway car in the forest of Compiegne, north of Paris. The final casualty statistics for the war shocked the world. There were 10 million dead, 20 million wounded in battle and 5 million dead due to starvation and disease. The direct cost of the war was 337 billion dollars.[2]

More Recognition for Newfoundland Regiment

With the Armistice signed and the Allied forces making preparations for its enforcement, two more honours were bestowed on the Royal Newfoundland Regiment. Britain had assigned two of its armies to the role of occupational forces on the Rhine in the area between Cologne and Dusseldorf. The outstanding battlefield performance of the 9th Division, which included the Newfoundland Regiment, had impressed British military leaders so much, that they assigned part of this occupation-force role to the 9th Division under General Sir Hugh Tudor.

The march to the Rhine began on November 14th, and it took the division three weeks to cross Belgium. It was while crossing Belgium that the Newfoundland Regiment was again recognized. One hundred soldiers from the Regiment were selected to

---

[2] The Twentieth Century, an Almanac.

represent all the colonial and dominion troops of the British Empire in a special parade to welcome King Albert's return to Brussel's, Belgium's capital.

On December 4th, the Highland Pipe Band playing "Blue Bonnets over the Border", were followed by the Royal Newfoundland Regiment, leading the 9th Division across the frontier heading for their assignment on the Rhine. Their reception on German soil was a far cry from the boisterous cheers that had greeted them in Brussels. A fearful German population, uncertain of their future and perhaps fearful and suspicious of foreign troops on their soil, remained in doors peeping out from behind curtains.

On December 13th, in pouring rain, the Royal Newfoundland Regiment crossed the Rhine. The news that greeted them on December 15th, sparked immediate cheering and celebrations. Their comrade-in-arms, Tommy Ricketts, had been awarded the Victoria Cross. Young Ricketts was overwhelmed with hand-shaking, congratulations and toasts to his health were drunk with German beer, the only available liquor at the time.

During the Christmas night celebrations, an unknown soldier or soldiers paid a visit to the statue of Bismarck standing in the town square at Hilden. The next morning the citizens of the town were dismayed to see that Bismarck was wearing a British Army greatcoat and a tin hat.

The Regiment's long road home began in February 1919 when they were moved to France and, in April, were given leave to visit the United Kingdom. Presented with multiple places to choose from, the majority chose Scotland where they had trained.

In their last weeks in London, the Royal Newfoundland Regiment participated in the march of the Colonial and Dominion troops in the Victory Parade in London on May 3rd. On that day, King George paid special tribute to the Regiment for its outstanding performance at Monchy-le-Preux, France, a crucial battle of the war.

The last social event for the Regiment before leaving England for home was a reunion dinner held at the Café Royal on Regent Street where Newfoundlanders had frequently met while on leave in London. On May 22nd, a full Newfoundland Battalion boarded the HMS *Corsica* for their trip home. Many of them were accompanied by their 'war brides.'

Despite the torrential rainstorm raging upon their arrival at Shea's Wharf in St. John's Harbour, a large and enthusiastic crowd had gathered to welcome them. The terrible weather did not deter the Regiment from performing its last duties, a march to Government House. They were greeted there by Governor Sir Alexander Harris who took custody of the Regimental colours. That event was followed by a banquet at the skating rink hosted by the women of St. John's.

To assure that those troops from outport Newfoundland were not delayed in getting to their homes, additional trains were made available by the Reid Newfoundland Railway. On July 1st, the final draft of soldiers was brought home by the *Cassandra*. Those too sick to travel were returned to Newfoundland at a later date.

Although the war came to an end in 1918, it did not bring an end to the enormous death and suffering. In the last days of WWI, The Spanish Flu had run its course, killing twice as many people as had died in the war. One third of the population of Labrador, including half the Inuit population, became victims of the pandemic. The coming on of winter saved Newfoundland from the destruction of life that had swept so many other countries. A vaccine for the Spanish Flu was not discovered until 1933.

Peace Conference

In January 1919, the Paris Peace Conference was held which drafted the Treaty of Versailles. The conditions under which it operated and the terms it imposed on Germany came back to haunt the world twenty years later. Although thirty-two countries participated in the conference and contributed to the terms to be imposed on Germany, Germany was excluded from attending. Conditions which Germany found impossible to fulfil were forced upon it. This proved to be another contribution to the rise of Hitler, who was able to argue that Germany had been betrayed by its politicians who readily accepted the full terms of the treaty.

The Peace Conference marked the first time in an international meeting that British Dominions were recognized as full members.[3] However, at the insistence of the United States, the list of Dominions was not given equal status with other countries in signing the armistice. Instead, the names of the Dominions

---

[3] Ibid.

WWI Victory Parade coming down Job Street, St. John's, Newfoundland, 1918. (PANL)

were indented on the list to that of Great Britain. Newfoundland was excluded because of its colonial status.

Brought Guns Home

Newfoundland soldiers returning home after the war, brought with them 'trophies of war.' British military policy was to hand over guns captured by a fighting force to that force once its claim was validated. Included in the trophies returned to Newfoundland were: 500 German rifles, five machine guns, and several field guns.

Other items, added later were meant to become part of a war museum or displayed in a public place. Up to the 1960s, some of the field guns were positioned in Bowring Park, Victoria Park and Bannerman Park.

A unique item returned from the battlefront was a war tank. Because the tank was invented by Winston Churchill and first used on the battlefield in 1916, it would today be a truly historic military artifact. However, it fell into the hands of a private individual, a garage owner, who kept it operating for years. It became the City of St. John's first motorized snowplough around 1922 when the owner contracted with the city to clear Water Street of snow. On the morning the snowploughing service was launched, hundreds

Newfoundland's National War Memorial was unveiled on July 1, 1924, by Field Marshal Earl Haig. The week was marked by a series of celebrations. (PANL)

turned up near the Court House at 6:00 a.m. to witness the event. However, the operator had problems starting it and this historic event was rescheduled for the next day. It was not in service very long because the inside chamber filled with fumes and almost suffocated the driver.

After its service as a snowplough, the tank was parked at the western side of the Court House on Water Street where it remained for years. When WWII broke out, it was converted into scrap metal for the war effort.

Expressions of Public Gratitude

It did not take long after the troops returned home for the public to begin showing their gratitude to the soldiers. December 1921, the first in a series of 'War Memorials' began to surface all over Newfoundland. The following is a list of these memorials.

St. Bon's College: January 12, 1921, by Governor Alexander Harris.

Sons of England Rooms, St. John's: May 22, 1921, Premier Sir Richard Squires.

The Kirk, St. John's: June 12, 1921, Governor Alexander Harris.

Sergeant's War Memorial,* St. John's: June 3, 1921, by Governor Alexander Harris.

Arnold's Cove, Placentia Bay: August 7, 1921.

Trinity, September 9, 1921.

Seal Cove, White Bay: November 7, 1921, Ricketts V.C. Memorial School opened and tablet unveiled by Dr. W.W. Blackall.

Church of England Institute: November 10, 1921, by Canon G. H. Bolt.

Bell Island, St. Boniface, Church of England, to Church Lads Brigade Cadets, by Rev. J. Stead, November 18, 1921.

Carbonear, November 13, 1921, by Rev. Mark Fenwick, President of the Methodist Conference.

Harbour Grace: at the Kirk, December 11, 1921, by Duguld Munn.

St. Mary's Church at St. John's: December 11, 1921, by Governor Alexander Harris.

St. Thomas' Church, January 23, 1922, by Bishop White.

Harvey & Co's: February 20, 1922, by Padres Clayton and Nangle.

Catholic Cadet Corps Armoury: March 22, 1922, by Lance-Corporal Longworth, youngest non commissioned officer in the Corps.

Gower Street United Church: May 21, 1922, by Governor Alexander Harris.

S.U.F. Hall at St. John's: June 2, 1922, by P.W. Phillips.

British Hall at St. John's: June 30, 1922, by Rev. Capt. Clayton.

Grand Falls: July 23, 1922, opened by Governor Alexander Harris.

Topsail: August 9, 1922, by Governor Alexander Harris.

Amiens Cathedral: August 27, 1922, by Premier Sir Richard Squires.

Bowring Park: September 13, 1922, *The Fighting Newfoundlander,* by Chief Justice Sir William Horwood.

Knights of Columbus School, St. John's, October 12, 1922, by Archbishop Roche.[4]

---

[4] H.M. Mosdell, When Was That?

The Sergeants' War Memorial was officially opened at the intersection of Queen's Road and Cathedral Street, St. John's, by Governor Alexander Harris on June 3, 1921. The area was once used as a place where the Newfoundland Justice System publicly administered punishments to criminals. The area had stocks, and a whirligig. People locked in the stocks and whirligig sometimes had mud thrown in their faces by townspeople.

British troops on the Somme. (IWA)

The War Memorial on Water Street in St. John's was unveiled by Field Marshall Earl Haig on Tuesday, July 1, 1924. It was built to honour the memory of Newfound-landers killed in World War I. The opening took place on the anniversary date of the Battle of the Somme which occurred on July 1, 1916. It was at that famous battle that the Newfoundland Regiment earned the title Royal.

In older times, other battles were fought near this site. The regular Sunday fisticuffs among the Irish youth gangs sometimes took place in this area, as well as up at the Parade Grounds which were in an area off the east side of Parade Street behind the CLB Armoury Building on Harvey Road. On one occasion a mounted military force were sent to both areas after the fighting got out of hand and spread to other parts of the city.[5]

On September 22, 1942, an unusual robbery took place at the War Memorial. Someone stole the bayonet from the hand of the soldier's figure. A naval craftsman in the city was called upon to make a new one and to repair the damage to the statue caused by the removal of the original. His work was very professional and the damaged section, when repaired, was unrecognizable.

---

[5] Jack Fitzgerald, Remarkable Stories of Newfoundland, Creative Publishers.

Imperial Awards

At the end of the war, the British Government presented a special award to the next of kin of those who died in the war. The honour was in the form of a Memorial Plaque of bronze and a Memorial Scroll. The Memorial Plaque was made in London and the information for the scroll was obtained from the Regiment and put on it by F.B. Burridge of the London County Central School of Arts and Crafts.

The British Imperial War Graves Commission looked after the care of graves of fallen soldiers in the United Kingdom and in the different theatres of war. A standard size headstone was erected on the grave of each fallen soldier. The Newfoundland Government contributed $5000 for this purpose. Many Newfoundlanders were buried in Brookwood Cemetery, near London, which turned into a military cemetery. A large monument was erected there in memory of all the soldiers buried there.

Regimental History Preserved on Film

During WWI, film production companies, then known as 'cinematograph companies,' made films of the various units of the Newfoundland Regiment for propaganda purposes. Some of these were kept by the Department of Militia, and the Provincial Archives of Newfoundland have most of those that survived.

The films included: the 2nd Battalion in training at Ayr and Barry, Scotland and Winchester, England; The 1st Battalion in France; The Forestry Corps at work during the summer and winter; The 3rd London General Hospital where many of the Regiment's wounded were treated; The Perth Hospital where foresters needing medical care were treated; Films of the Regiment in Aldershot and in St. John's were also available, but in 1919 they were not the property of the Newfoundland Government.

The Scots still have 1914 "Caribou Head"

Governor Davidson was moved by the friendliness and kindness of the people of Ayr, Scotland towards the Newfoundland soldiers and he decided to show them Newfoundland's appreciation. During the summer of 1916, Davidson instructed the Hon. S. D. Blandford, Minister of Agriculture in New-foundland, to secure a caribou head and have it mounted. Davidson told the Provost of Ayr (Scottish Mayor), "A caribou head

The Caribou Head as it is today in storage in a museum in Scotland. (Paul Sweeney)

The presentation of a caribou head to the burgh of Ayr, Scotland was a celebrated event in 1916. Newfoundland's Prime Minister Sir Edward Morris and his wife went to Scotland for the presentation. (L-R) Prime Minister Morris, the Mayor of Ayr and Lady Morris. Officers of the Newfoundland Regiment are included in the picture. (PANL)

is the most typical trophy of sport in Newfoundland." It was also the emblem of the Newfoundland Regiment and was rapidly growing in stature among Allied troops due to the Regiment's accomplishments in Gallipoli and France. Describing the head to the Provost, the Governor pointed out:

> This head, judged by the spread and weight of the antlers and the number of points on the tines, is an exceptionally fine specimen of the caribou, trophies of such proportions being extremely rare. My ministers express the hope that you, Mr. Provost, may be able to find space for the gift from the loyal and ancient Colony in the Burgh Hall, as a souvenir of the gratitude of all Newfoundlanders for the kindness rendered to their fighting men by the Royal Burgh of Ayr.[6]

The Provost arranged to put the gift on public display in the shop window of Robert Wallace, Ltd., Town Buildings. It remained

---

[6] Ayr Museum. Minutes of Burgh Meeting, August 1916. File of Provost of the Royal Burgh of Ayr, Scotland, 1916.

204   THE SPRING RICE DOCUMENT

in Ayr on public display for decades after the war but then it appears to have been forgotten. Brothers, Paul and Stephen Sweeney, while researching in Scotland during February 2011, for author Jack Fitzgerald, traced the Caribou to the "Rozelle House Galleries, Ayr." Rozelle House is the new home to South Ayrshire Council's permanent art and museum collection and a most popular visiting place for tourists to the city. The Sweeney's traced the historic Caribou Head to Rozelle House where it is currently preserved in the Museum's storage area and in very good shape.

Graves of Newfoundland Soldiers Buried in Scotland

The following is a list of members of the Royal Newfoundland Regiment wounded in Battle and who succumbed to injuries while being treated in Scotland:

List "A" is made up of the names of twelve soldiers and the name of the cemetery where each is buried.

List "B" is of the fourteen Regiment soldiers who are all buried in the Ayr Cemetery.

The author is most grateful to brothers Paul and Stephen Sweeney for their contribution in researching and compiling the information below. The Sweeney's are from Glasgow, about forty miles from Ayr. Paul Sweeney is now a permanent resident of St. John's and Stephen is resident of Glasgow.

List "A"

Name	Date/Cemetery
Pte. J. F. Chaplin	January 1, 1915 Ardersier-Invernesshire
Pte. J. J. Gorman	March 30, 1915 MountVernon-Edinburgh
Pte. J. H. Thorne	February 21, 1916 Hawkhead Cemetery Paisley
Pte G. Mugford	February 24, 1916 Hawkhead Cemetery Paisley
Pte. James Ford	February 2, 1916 Hawkhead Cemetery Paisley

This well kept grave site at Ayr, Scotland is the burial place of fourteen Newfoundland soldiers who died in Scotland from wounds received in battle. The names and burial sites of another twelve soldiers is recorded on the tombstone in the centre-front. These sites are in nine other cemeteries in Scotland. (Paul Sweeney)

Sgt. G. Dick   December 17, 1916
                                Largs, Ayreshire

Pte. P.J. Boland   December 21, 1916
                                Sannox, Isle of Arran

Bdsmn. W. Maddock   March 17, 1917
                                Cathcart Cemetery Glasgow

L.Cpl. C. Hunt   June 7, 1917
                                Western Cemetery Glasgow

Pte. S. Taylor   March 9, 1918
                                Dunkeld, Perthshire

Pte. G. Hogan   August 16, 1918
                                Kenmore, Aberfeldy

Pte. A.H. Wyatt   December 10, 1918
                         Kenmore, Aberfeldy

List "B"
Members of the Royal Newfoundland Regiment who are buried in
well kept graves in the Ayr Cemetery, Scotland:

Name	Date/Age
Pte. P. Rideout	April 27 1918 / 24.
Pte. J. D. Doody	February 4th 1918 / 25
Pte. A. Fitzpatrick	January 29 1916 / 18
Sgt. P. F. Tobin	December 27 1916 / 21
Pte. Stephen J. Paul	March 20, 1917 / N/A
H. Hare	May 25 1916 / 17
H. Smith	June 3 1916 / 21
V. P. Newell	July 17, 1917 / 19
H. Hulan	May 2, 1916 / 18
J. Lambert	April 7, 1916 / 23
John T. Tobin	February 1, 1916 / 19
James O'Brien	October 2, 1915 / 22
P. J. Constantine	April 8, 1920 / 21
A. Roberts	November 1st / 24

Paul Sweeney and his brother Stephen, searched museums and graveyards in Scotland to provide author Jack Fitzgerald, with material on the missing "Caribou Head" of 1914 and the burial sites of members of the Newfoundland Regiment who died in Scotland as the result of wounds received in battle. (Submitted photos)

Chapter 9

WWI MISCELLANY

Superstitions on the Battlefront

After fighting on fronts in Gallipoli and France, the Newfoundlanders had some new wartime superstitions to add to those they already held. The most widespread superstition surrounded the number three. The third of anything was believed to be fatal. Consequently, soldiers were concerned about their third leaves. Some even refused to take the third leave because they felt they would be killed upon returning to the front.

Lighting three cigarettes using the one match was the basis of another popular superstition. They believed that one of the three soldiers, sharing a match, was bound to be killed within weeks, and even those watching the sharing of one match would experience bad luck. In WWII a different belief surrounded using one match to light three cigarettes. Soldiers reasoned that by the time the match was used to light the third cigarette, a sniper had time to take aim on the source of the light.

British gunners usually spit on their shells before firing them in battle. Many who witnessed the practice found it amusing, but it was actually seen by the soldier as an act of sacrifice of great antiquity. In ancient times, people believed that saliva was part of the soul of the individual, and to part with it in the act of spitting was tantamount to making a sacrifice. There was an old-time practice of Newfoundland fishermen to spit into the mouth of the first fish of the fishing season as an offering in hope for a successful season.

Prior to WWI, all the odd numbers, except thirteen, were supposed to be lucky, especially seven and nine. With the breakout of war, this changed and all odd numbers were considered unlucky. Friday used to be considered an unlucky day, but Sunday was a very lucky day on which to go into battle.

Perhaps taken from the Scots was the practice of tucking white heather in the bands of the cap which was believed to protect the wearer from a fatal wound.

There was a strong sense of fatalism among the troops. For example, it was common for soldiers to say, "If a bullet is not made for you, you will come through all right."

Strangely, when compared to today's superstitions, all armies viewed a black cat as an omen of the greatest good luck. A cuckoo's call before breakfast was a sign of bad luck.

A bizarre superstition was associated with the introduction of submarine warfare in WWI because it increased the risk to life at sea. This required having possession of a "caul" which was a traditional charm against loss of life at sea. A caul is the membrane containing fluid, occasionally found on a baby's head at birth. This was thought to be an infallible amulet against death by drowning.

The *Evening Telegram* on June 12, 1918, reported, "At many places around the docks in the great European ports, one can see the little signs, 'A Child's Caul for sale,' and fancy figures are demanded for them."

Eerie Appearance on a Battlefield

History has recorded two strange and amazing connections between the battlefield and scarlet red poppies, long before these flowers became the remembrance poppies for war veterans.

The first occurred in the Battle of Landen, Netherlands, in 1693 between the French Army and the British under King William III. In that battle, more than 20,000 men were killed and left unburied on the field. One year later, the field erupted into millions and millions of scarlet red poppies covering the entire battlefront as if with a vast sheet of blood.

The second event took place in 1798 in the same area following the Victory at Waterloo when the entire battlefield broke out into a blaze of scarlet red poppies.[1]

The Somme had been a Battlefield for hundreds of Years

An article in the *Evening Telegram* on October 17, 1918, referring to the Somme battlefield in France, stated, "It is a fitting fight for world freedom in the 'Cockpit of Europe' which for more than a thousand years has been the scene of epoch making battles. There is scarcely a foot on all the long battlefront of France that has not echoed to the tramp of army boots."

---

[1]The Evening Telegram, October 18, 1918, p9.

At St. Quinton in 1871, the Germans under Von Goeben defeated the French.

In 1870 at Amiens the Germans defeated the French.

In 1814, near Rheims, where French Kings were coronated, Napoleon defeated Russia.

In 1814, at St. Quinton, the British defeated the French.

In 1794 at Ypres area, the French defeated the Austrians.

The article noted that King Louis XV captured Lille in 1792 and strongly defended it against an Austrian army.

In 1684, Somme was the scene of a great battle in which France defeated Spain.

On August 10, 1557 the army of King Philip II achieved victory over France at St. Quinton.

In 1477, Charles the Bold was defeated at Nancy.

In 1302, the Flemish defeated the French Army at Courtrai. The French Army was twice the size of the Flemish.[2]

The Ayre Family telegram- July 13-1916

Everybody will read with pleasure the Royal message of sympathy from the King and Queen to Mr. Fred Ayre, which is, of course, a message to the three Ayre families. On few in Newfoundland has any blow of the war fallen with such terrific heaviness as upon the Ayres. Leading citizens of our town and country they have paid the highest price to our cause and have won a name throughout the Empire.

Ayre's Department Store on Water Street in the era of WWI. The site today is occupied by Atlantic Place. (City of St. John's Archives)

All of their four sons, Gerald, Eric, Bernard and Wilfred, were killed in battle. Their Majesties words came from them personally; they are worth many a coveted distinction.

The Royal Cable read:

The King and Queen have heard with much regret of the death of the four members of your

---

[2] The Evening Telegram, October 17, 1918.

family whilst gallantly fighting in France. Their Majesties deplore the loss which you and the Colony of Newfoundland have sustained by the death of these brave officers and truly sympathize with you in your sorrow.

— *Signed*— *Keeper of the Privy Purse*

From *The Evening Telegram* July 1916
The Story of Their Heroic Part

With the Battle of the Somme progressing, the heroism of Newfoundlanders in the opening battle was being told at home: London-4:30 a.m. July 13, 1916.

The *Times* correspondent at the British Headquarters in France sends the following:

> The Newfoundlanders were the only overseas troops engaged in these operations. The story of their heroic part cannot yet be told in full, but when it is, it will make Newfoundland very proud. The Battalion pushed up to what may be called the third wave in the attack, probably the most formidable section of the whole German front, through an almost overwhelming artillery fire across the ground, which was swept by enfilading machine-gun fire from hidden positions. The men behaved with completely noble steadiness and courage.

Tribute from Montreal

Special from Montreal's *Star* Newspaper Correspondent:

> Stirring accounts of the heroism of the Newfoundland Regiment appear in the London press today. They advanced in a hail of German lead as calmly as on parade. One private says that as he was going by another said, 'If I go down, you take up the charge and go straight ahead...' A minute afterwards he dropped. 'I tried to lift him up, but he was done for. His last words were: 'Push on with it.'

The Evening Telegram Editorial- July 13, 1916

"Push on with it!" *The Evening Telegram* reported, "should become household words in Newfoundland." The newspaper added to the stories out of London:

Our men have won another distinction– that of being the only overseas troops to participate with their British kinsmen in the memorable engagement. Britain's oldest colony would ask no higher an honour.

At the Dardanelles, our boys came to know the Anzacs, [Australians and New Zealanders] and cemented a bond of comradeship that will for long link us with far away Australia and New Zealand, hitherto, mere names to us. But now they have swept into their real heritage. They swept forward side by side with the men from "home.' It is not alone Newfoundland that has occasion to feel very proud. We have always known and remembered our mother: Britain will now recognize their sons.

Royal Navy Reserve

In comparison to the Newfoundland Regiment, very little has been written about those Newfoundlanders who served in the Royal Navy during WWI. Unlike their brother Newfoundlanders in the Regiment, the Navy volunteers were spread throughout the Royal Navy, and their story is part of the glorious story of the British Navy. Yet, their abilities certainly did not go unnoticed by senior Royal Navy officers. Governor Davidson summed up the praise he was receiving from the British Admiralty regarding their performance in a communication he sent to Colonial Secretary, John Bennett. Davidson stated:

Reservists from Newfoundland have a very high reputation for seamanship, steadiness and character. Furthermore, Naval Officers look after them with special care, in view of the fact that they cannot take home-leave and are volunteers for the purpose of the war only.[3]

Regatta Nostalgia at Beaumont Hamel

There was a heightened sense of a pending war at the Regatta of 1914. Throughout the day committee member Harold Jeans kept the crowds informed on events in Europe which led to Britain's declaration of war on Germany. Patriotism at lakeside was

---

[3] PANL GN 1/3/A Box 97 Files 1-95.

so high that when the Governor arrived at the Regatta, the crowds spontaneously burst into the singing of the "Ode To Newfoundland" followed by "Rule Britannia".

Among those present that day was Regatta legend Sam Ebsary who in recent years was inducted into the Royal St. John's Regatta Hall of Fame. He was one of the First Five Hundred volunteers, better known as the Blue Puttees.

One of the Regatta's all-time great coxswains, Sam Ebsary, quickly moved up in rank from Sergeant to Second Lieutenant with the Royal Newfoundland Regiment. He was among the few that survived the Battle of Beaumont Hamel on July 1, 1916. Sombre, heartsick days followed the disaster. Ebsary often thought of home and that, if war had not broken out, crowds would at that time be at Quidi Vidi watching crews practice for the Regatta.[4]

During this period an incident took place that reflected the depth of love Newfoundlanders hold for the traditional Regatta at Quidi Vidi. Darkness had fallen over the land and soldiers were sitting around at the camp-type headquarters quietly reflecting upon the recent tragedies. *The Fighting Newfoundlander* described what happened that night. Colonel Nicholson wrote:

It was nearly midnight when 2nd Lieutenant Sam Ebsary dropped out of the darkness near the entrance to re-appear with a large accordion which he had brought with him from 'A' Company's billets in the ramparts.

Let one of 'D' Company's officers who was present describe the scene: 'Sitting in the corner on an empty ammunition box, he commenced to play and as the music emerged from the instrument, the sand-bagged walls of our 'HQ' seemed to fade; 'The Banks of Newfoundland' rang in our ears, and we saw once more the tented slopes of Quidi Vidi on Regatta Day; the Blue Peter had turned the buoy and the other boats were swinging into position.' Less than three months later on October 12, 1916 Sam Ebsary died from wounds received in the Battle of Guedecourt.

---

[4] Jack Fitzgerald, A Day at the Races, Creative Publishers.

His career at the Regatta ran from 1899 to 1913. During this period, he participated in every Regatta with a total of seventy-one races which included thirty-four wins; twenty-two second place spots and eight third place finishes. He was also respected as the Regatta's top coxswain of that era. Little wonder that about twenty-five years later a Newfoundlander speaking to a gathering at Cape Breton compared how Newfoundlanders feel about the St. John's Regatta by stating, "It's our Grecian Olympics, our American 4th of July all combined into one day."[5]

Germans at the Races

Ironically, just thirteen years before the battlefront death of Ebsary, German soldiers were welcomed at the St. John's Regatta and participated in a boating competition against rowers from the British Navy and a crew of young cadets from St. John's.

The people of St. John's were accustomed to seeing British Navy crews compete at the historic Quidi Vidi Regatta but a rowing crew from the German Navy was another matter. When it was announced in 1903 that the German Navy would be entering a crew in the Naval-Brigade Race at the Regatta, enthusiasm soared. People speculated on how the Germans would do against local rowers or the crew that year from the British Navy.

The German entry came as a welcome surprise to the people of St. John's. The German Naval Gunboat, *Panther*, arrived in St. John's Harbour to take on supplies, days before the Regatta. When they learned of the historic Regatta being held near the city and that the British Navy was participating, they eagerly accepted an invitation to participate.

Three crews competed in the Naval-Brigade Race: the British, the Germans and a crew with the top rowers taken from the Church Lads Brigade and the Catholic Cadet Corps. The Germans were assigned the Blue Peter, the fastest boat on the pond and gambling on the race was widespread. Even the German and British Naval Officers waged bets on the outcome. However, it soon became evident after the starting gun fired that the British were the crew to beat. They crossed over the finish line with the CLB-CCC crews in second place and the Germans a distant last.

---

[5] Ibid.

Nevertheless, the Germans were good sports and stayed at lakeside to enjoy the races. The Panther's Brass Band enthusiastically took over music duties from Professor Power's Band in the afternoon to allow the local band members time to participate in the festive activities at lakeside.

The Fighting Newfoundlander Remains in England

The statue of 'The Fighting Newfoundlander' in Bowring Park is not the original. Sculpted by the renowned artist Basil Gotto in 1918, the original remains in England. The Bowring Park statue is a bronze replica of the original work and was donated to the City of St. John's by Sir Edgar Bowring in 1922. The original was also purchased by the Bowring family.

The man who posed for the statue was Thomas Pittman, D.C.M, and M.M, who passed away in St. John's on April 10, 1966 at the age of seventy-seven. Pittman was among the 250 members of the Royal Newfoundland Regiment who left St. John's for overseas during the fall of 1915. Pittman was wounded four times and decorated twice. He was awarded the Distinguished Conduct Medal and the Military Medal. He didn't go over the top during his first battle on July 1, 1916, being among the group held back for defensive purposes. When he did go over the top, he took four hits; one on the side of his head, the others piercing his shoulder and sides. He was treated by medics, and returned to the battlefront.

In 1918 he was stationed in Winchester, England, with the Royal Newfoundland Regiment. An officer there informed him that he was to go to the School of Arts to meet with the eminent sculptor Basil Gotto. The sculptor looked him over closely and then commented, "You'll do." Gotto began working on what has become one of Newfoundland's most famous monuments. For about two hours every day, for two months, Pittman held a pose while Gotto worked. Finally, the statue of a fighting man, with gas mask hanging off, grenade in one hand and rifle in the other, was completed. Pittman's comrades used to drop in at the studio to watch him pose. They would say to each other, "Let's go down and see the Fighting Newfoundlander," which is how the renowned statue got its name. Thomas Pittman, made famous by this statue, is buried in Mount Pleasant Cemetery in St. John's.

Forestry Units

By 1917, a serious need developed for workers to harvest the forests of England and Scotland due to the insatiable demands for lumber brought on by the war. In response to a request to the Newfoundland Regiment to supply trained lumbermen to work overseas, 500 men were recruited. These included some veterans who had been discharged at Gallipoli and France.

On May 19, 1917, the first group departed from St. John's for Scotland. Upon arrival, they were assigned to the forests of Dunkeld and Blairgowrie. As overseas loggers, the men were all members of the Royal Newfoundland Regiment.

Don't Tell Us

In 1916, during WWI, the Ladies Patriotic Association of Harbour Grace held a "Soup Sociable" at St. Paul's Hall on March 3rd to raise funds for their projects to help our soldiers overseas. At least one person in the community wasn't happy with the menu. Using the pseudonym 'Sunny Jim', probably Jimmy Murphy,[6] he published a letter and poem in the *Evening Telegram* on March 4th showing his discontent. He wrote, "The mussel vendors are doing good business in their line just now, and there is ready sale for the shell fish at 15 cents a bucket."

> Don't tell us that you're down to soup
> And mussels in the second city,
> If that be so, there are other mates
> Than Poles and Serbs deserving pity.
>
> It makes us think that submarines
> Hang round the Isle of Carbonearo,
> That mines are round about you flung
> Until your hearts are down to zero.
>
> That you can't walk up to Stretten's Hill
> With your good wife or maiden tender,
> But you're confronted by a Hun
> Who cries in stertorous tones "Surrender!"

---

[6] Jimmy Murphy worked with the Bard of Prescott Street Johnny Burke in writing songs and ballads, and himself produced volumes. Both sold song sheets on the streets of St. John's for pennies.

It sounds like news from hemmed Berlin,
Or like the news we're primed for hearing,
For this you will be censored Bill,
For such bad news is well nigh scaring.

Tell us some stuff to take our minds
Far, far away from Europe's tussels
But don't go tell us that you're forced
In Harbour Grace to soup and mussels.

The Navy Reserve Short Changed

It was brought to Government's attention in February 1918 that the members of the Royal Naval Reserve were being paid at a lower rate than the men of the Newfoundland Regiment. The Militia Department moved immediately to bring the Reserve up to par with the Regiment. Although it was not the Militia Department's responsibility to handle Royal Naval Reserve matters, to expedite the issue, it accepted the responsibility immediately.

This matter, in addition to handling the payment of civilian clothing allowances to the Reserves, required that the Department increase the staff of its Pay Office and it augmented the duties of these officials.

Invented the Gas Mask

During the Second Battle of Ypres on the Western Front, both sides were taking heavy casualties. However, this time the Germans introduced a new horror on the battlefield when they began their attack using gas. It was April 25, 1915, and the gas killed thousands of soldiers who died horrible deaths. The British rapidly responded with a new invention called 'the gas mask.' The man who invented it was St. John's born Cluny Macpherson, serving as Lt.-Col. with the Newfoundland Regiment in Scotland at the time. The mask was placed over the entire head before the helmet was put on. It was made of a khaki flannel cloth using a film material as an eye opening. Improvements to the invention soon followed. In recognition of his contribution he was awarded the Companion of the Order of St. Michael and St. George, Mentioned in Dispatches, and received Honourable Mention to Secretary of State for War.

The WWI Flying Suit had a NL Connection

Sidney Cotton was born in Australia and fought with the Royal Navy Air Services during WWI. He moved to Newfoundland in 1920 and in the years leading up to WWII worked for British and French Intelligence.

However, in 1916 he invented the layered flying suit called the Sidcot suit which was adopted around the world and used by pilots during the war. Even the German War Ace Baron von Richtofen was wearing a Sidcot Suit when he was shot down. Cotton refused to accept any payment for his invention.

In Newfoundland, he was the first to use an aircraft for delivering mail to communities isolated during winter months. He was the first to use an aircraft to search out large areas of timber on the island, and was also the first to utilize aerial photography to make aerial maps. He was even the first to use air search to locate seal herds at the icefields.

As a spy, he posed as a private businessman and secretly equipped his plane with remote controlled cameras on the wings to photograph military establishments in Germany and the Middle East.

While in Newfoundland, he used his genius to invent a cover to keep the aircraft engine warm in cold weather. He used catalytic lamps under the aircraft's engine to prevent engine freezing, and equipped the aircraft with special winter survival gear.

Money Disadvantage

For most of the war, families of the men serving overseas, and their sons, brothers and husbands, were being short-changed every time they sent money by cable-transfer overseas. Relatives and friends were sending money to the men overseas through the banks and cable offices and, consequently, losing the exchange in Newfoundland as well as in the United Kingdom. The new Department of Militia, in the fall of 1917, moved to change this. It adopted the policy which enabled monies to be sent at a minimum cost, and the soldier to receive the amount at par.

At the same time, the Department approved the payment of Separation Allowance to dependents of members of the Newfoundland Regiment and Forestry Corps. The allowance was, at first, retroactive to September 1, 1917, but it was later changed and made retroactive from the date of enlistment.

War-Bread

During WWI, while many Newfoundlanders risked their lives overseas in the fight for freedom, people at home were called upon to make sacrifices. Among those sacrifices was bread. The military had first claim on the best flour and other necessities. Bakers and housewives had to improvise to make bread to feed their families.

During March 1918, a "war bread exhibition" took place at British Hall. Four classes of bread were featured in the exhibition. They included bread made from: wheat, flour, and potatoes; wheat flour and oatmeal; wheat flour and corn; wheat flour and a mix of all other ingredients.

The purpose of the exhibition was to highlight the need for economy in the use of flour.

Military Composer from St. John's

During World War II, Canadian military bands played march music composed by Newfoundland born Private Harold Noseworthy. His most famous work was "Fiery Chariots" which he dedicated to the Canadian Armoured Corps. Another march composed by Noseworthy after he was wounded during WWI was 'The Battle of the Somme.' He was one of sixty-six survivors of his battalion at that battle.

The Fiery Chariots was built around the Regimental call of the Tank Corps, and contains representation of bursts of machine and anti-tank guns, done by percussion instruments with clarinets and saxophones. In place, the reed section of the band portrayed the scream of shells.

Harold Noseworthy was born in St. John's, NL, in 1896. He played his first solo in public at the age of four. While serving with the CLB Band 1919 to 1922, he wrote a march called, "Colonel Rendell" which he dedicated to the Commander of the CLB. In 1923, he married Mabel Bates and they moved to Marshal Town, Indiana.

In 1934 the Noseworthys took their three sons and moved back to Newfoundland. In 1944 their three sons enlisted with the United States Navy and fought in many sea battles. Noseworthy, himself, served with the Canadian Veterans' Guard Band.

Harold Noseworthy was the first Canadian to complete tests in Toronto for the degree awarded by the College of Music, London,

England. He also studied harmony and orchestration at Chicago Extension Conservatory.

First American Volunteer a Newfoundlander

Dr. William B. Giles was a noted medical doctor in the United States and Argentina. He was born in St. John's, the son of Captain Edward J. Giles, a former master of the Red Cross liner *Sylvia*. Giles held impressive medical credentials. He was a graduate of Harvard Medical Postgraduate School, Tufts Medical College and the New York Poly-Clinic Postgraduate School.

This St. John's native was one of the first volunteers sent by the United States Army to France during WWI. He served there as surgeon to a French military hospital and later served on a US Navy hospital ship.

After the war, Dr. Giles went to Argentina on an American Observation tour and decided to stay there. During his career in Argentina, he was recognized as one of the country's finest doctors. Giles, before going to Argentina, taught at Bellevue Medical, NY and was attached to the Children's Hospital, and the West Side Hospital in New York.

British Hoax Worked

In 1914 German Intelligence was baffled over reports that the battleship HMS *Audacious*, which by accounts from witnesses had been sent to the bottom of the sea off Northern Ireland after striking a German mine, was fully restored and ready again to do battle.

Not only the Germans, but passengers on the White Star liner *Olympic* travelling from Liverpool to the United States in October, witnessed the ship about to go under. They arrived in time to see a British cruiser and several destroyers standing by to take on survivors.

Captain H. J. Haddock, the *Olympic's* captain, had altered his course after receiving a distress single from the *Audacious*. Author Richard Garrett stated:

> In a brave effort which, had it come off, would have made naval history, Captain Haddock tried to take the battleship in tow. One attempt followed another, and, each time, the hawser snapped. Finally, at four o'clock in the afternoon,

Captain Haddock was compelled to give up. However, he continued to stand by the mortally wounded warship, and presently some of her crew were transferred to the liner. The passengers gathered eagerly round them.[7]

Two passengers present at the time were astounded when, on a return trip to England after the war, they met a Scotsman who claimed he had seen the battleship many times at Lock Ewe and Scapa Flow in Scotland. The Americans showed the Scot pictures of the battleship as she was about to sink. Both parties were mystified and began to discuss the possibility of ghost ships. However, the incident had nothing to do with the supernatural. In fact, it was an ingenious hoax perpetuated by Winston Churchill.

As Lord of the Admiralty, Churchill wanted to convince the Germans that the British navy was vastly superior to the Imperial German Navy and, as well, to impress the Turks who were about to make an alliance with Germany. Churchill was convinced that the loss of a major battleship such as *Audacious* would harm England's prestige. He set in motion a plan to create a duplicate, in appearances, at least, of the sunken battleship.

Churchill tracked down an eighteen-year-old Canadian Pacific liner named the *Montcalm* and had it requisitioned. He put a team of craftsmen and carpenters to work and supplied them with whatever wood, paint and canvas needed to make the ship look like the *Audacious*. When finished, even seasoned British seamen couldn't tell the difference.

His plan was to show her now and then, but keep her away from any possibility of confrontation. The vessel was docked at Loch Ewe in the North West of Scotland where she remained anchored most of the time. Churchill's deception fooled German Intelligence who firmly believed that this major battleship in Scotland was ready to repel any enemy action off that country's coast.

This story has an ironic twist. Captain Haddock, who worked desperately to save the *Audacious* from sinking, was the only one of the many witnesses who knew Churchill's secret. Soon after he had arrived in New York with the *Olympia,* he joined the Royal

---

[7] Richard Haddock, <u>Great Sea Mysteries</u>, London, 1954.

Navy. His first assignment was to take command of the Churchill hoax project and see it to its completion.

Merchant Seamen in POW Camp in Germany

Samuel James Newell served as a crewman on the schooner *Jean* owned by Crosbie and Co. and torpedoed by a German submarine during the summer of 1918. Although the Germans usually made provisions for civilians taken from private vessels to be set free near a safe area, in this case, the crew was taken to Germany and imprisoned in the POW (Head) Camp at Gustrow, Mecklenburg, Newell, had a wife and young son living on Southside Road in St. John's. The following is a letter he sent to his wife, Elfreda at 2 Southside Road. It read:

Dear Wife, – It is with much pleasure that I sit down to answer your most kind and welcome letter which I received a few days ago, and was also glad to hear that you were all well, except my mother, and I am most sorry to hear that, but I hope she will be better by now. As for myself I am in the best of health and hoping you are the same.

You said James Efford is married to Lena Young. Things like that are happening every day. You can wish him much joy for me and tell him I will be home to see himself myself someday or another. You said, when I would get your letter, to write as quickly as possible and you would send me a box. I thank you for your kindness, but I'd sooner you would keep it until I come home, as I did not my boots and other things I had sent for.

And you can tell Gus Gullage to stay home and look after his wife and don't go away because he might become a prisoner like I am; and I wish all the young couples that are married, the best of joy in their future life, and I will be home to see the bride and groom some day.

Say, Elfreda, I am waiting for a letter from Lydia for quite awhile now, and I would also like to get one from Jessie, too. I think I have said all for this time. Remember me to all home. Give my love to my mother and tell her not to fret I will be home some day if God spares me to come. And also give my love to Skipper Joseph, Lydia and Jessie and to my little Georgie and my best love and respects for yourself. Nothing more at present from your ever loving husband.

(Sgd.) Samuel Jas. Newell. Late Schr. "Jean."[8]

Lamaline Man Encounters 'The Sea Devil'

Captain B. G. Hooper of Lamaline, Newfoundland, had an intriguing encounter with the famous German Count von Luckner, who was dubbed 'The Sea Devil' during WWI because of his military exploits.

'The Sea Devil' earned his reputation while in command of the German raider *Seadler*. During one three month period, the 'Sea Devil' took on board several hundred prisoners and among them was Captain B. Hooper. In 1916, Hooper had signed on the foreign-going, three-masted schooner *Pearce*. On his first trip, the delivery of a cargo of fish to Brazil, his ship was overtaken by von Luckner.

After taking all on board his vessel as prisoners, he ordered the sinking of the *Pearce*. The Germans were already carrying a load of prisoners. Hooper recalled later that the Sea Devil was a man of honour and lofty principles which he applied in war and peace. The prisoners were made as comfortable as possible in the ship's hold and were all treated well. When the vessel was not involved in a chase or combat, von Luckner allowed the prisoners to go on deck.

Hooper pointed out that discipline was rigid and they were obliged to work on deck. The Sea Devil also insisted that each prisoner be paid for any work carried out. Between January 24th and March 21, 1917, the Sea Devil captured eight ships and removed all crews and passengers before sinking them. When it became overcrowded, the Germans released some prisoners and allowed them to return home. Among those was Captain Hooper whom he released in a Brazilian Port.

After the war, Hooper became the Marine Superintendent for Dominion Steel and Coal Corporation on Bell Island. He credited

---

[8] The Evening Telegram, June 7, 1918.

von Luckner with teaching him much about the sea and being a sailor.

Small Battles Recognized

During WWI, the British Imperial Nomenclature Committee (INC) wrestled with the problem of appropriately designating the many battles fought by its forces while at the same time maintaining a manageable size listing. Often, smaller battles were recognized as part of a wider battle. These designations were crucial to the Battle Honours Committee which made their awards based on the INC's designations. According to historian, G.W. Nicholson:

> As a general rule, only those battles in which a substantial number of troops had taken part were recognized. Lesser engagements, important though each might be to the individual unit or units involved, had to be grouped under the designation of the larger operation of which they formed a part. There was one notable exception. Acknowledging the tremendous significance to Newfoundlanders of the name Beaumont Hamel, the authorities granted the Royal Newfoundland Regiment the unique honour "Albert (Beaumont Hamel)"– a "bracketing" of honours which was to provide an important precedent for a parallel form of award to certain Commonwealth units in the Second World War.[9]

Examples of the application of this bracketing are: the Regiment's fighting at the Steenbeek which formed part of the bigger Battle of Langemarck, and the Regiment's fighting at the Broembeek which is recognized in the wider Battle of Poelcappelle.

A Remaining Relic of WWI

A remarkable relic of WWI can still be viewed today in Curling, Bay of Islands on Newfoundland's west coast. There, near the site of the old Curling Jail House, stands an impressive rock wall which is 1000 feet in length, five feet high in some places and four feet

---

[9] G.W. Nicholson, The Fighting Newfoundlander.

deep. Many very large rocks went into the construction of this fence which was built by four German POWs being housed in the two cell jail.

These men were among the enemy aliens rounded up from ships in several ports around Newfoundland when war broke out. They were held at His Majesty's Penitentiary, at first, and after complaints about being housed with criminals, they were moved to jails in the outports. Later, the prisoners were transferred to the Donovan's POW Camp.

Inspector Isaac Bartlett of the Constabulary was in charge of the jail and appeared to have problems in finding appropriate daily recreation and physical activities to occupy the prisoner's time. Occasional volunteer chores were assigned for which the prisoners were compensated. Eventually, he arranged for them to work on his own private property nearby by clearing the property and undertaking the construction of the thousand feet long stone fence which provided Bartlett's property with a border. It was obvious, considering the small facilities and minimum staff, that the prisoners were trustworthy to be allowed so much time outside. It seems likely that they volunteered for the work.

BIBLIOGRAPHY

BOOKS

Abbatiello, John J. Anti-Submarine Warfare in World War I: British Naval Aviation and the Defeat of the U-Boats. London: Routeledge, Taylor and the Francis Group, 2006.

Bassler, Gerhard P. Vikings to U-Boats: The German Experience in Newfoundland and Labrador. Montreal: McGill-Queens University Press, 2006.

Cave, Joy. What Became of Corporal Pittman? St. John's: Breakwater Books, 1976.

Churchill, Winston. Great Contemporaries. London: Collins Clear-Type Press, 1937.

Facey-Crowther, Dr. David. Better Than the Best, The Royal Newfoundland Regiment. St. John's: The Royal Newfoundland Regiment Advisory Council, 1995.

Farrar-Hockley. The Somme. London: Pan Books, 1964.

Ferrell, Robert H. The Twentieth Century, an Almanc. New York: World Almanac Publications, 1984.

Fitzgerald, Jack. Jack Fitzgerald's Notebook. St. John's: Creative Book Publishing, 2002.

Fitzgerald, Jack. Strange but True Newfoundland Stories. St. John's: Creative Book Publishing, 1989

Garret, Richard. Great Sea Mysteries. London: Pan Books, 1971.

Harris, Brayton. The Navy Times Book of Submarines: a Political, Social and Military History. New York: Berkley Publishing Group, 1997.

Hart, B.H. The Real War 1914-1918. New York: Berkley Publishing Group, 1997.

Miller, David. U-Boats: History, Development and Equiptment, 1914-1945. England: Conway Maritime Press, 2000.

Morton, Desmond and Granatstein, J.L. Marching to Armageddon: Canadians and the Great War 1914-19. Toronto: Lester & Orpen Dennys Limited, 1989.

Murphy, Michael. Pathways to Yesterday. St. John's: Town Crier Publishing Company Ltd, 1976.

Nicholson, Colonel, G.W.L. A History of the Royal Newfoundland Regiment. Montreal: McGill University Press, 1964.

Pearson, John. The Private Lives of Winston Churchill. New York: Simon and Schuster, 1991.

Smallwood, Joseph R. The Encyclopedia of Newfoundland and Labrador. Vol. 3. St. John's: Newfoundland Book Publishers Ltd, 1981-1994

Smallwood, Joseph R. The Book of Newfoundland. 6 vols. St. John's: Newfoundland Book Publishers, 1937.

Stair-Gillon, Captain. The Story of the 29th Division. London:

Thomas Nelson & Sons Ltd, 1925.

Turdor, Sir Hugh. The Fog of War. [s.l. :bs.n.], 1959.

NEWSPAPERS & MAGAZINES

The Telegram. 1914-1920.

The Daily News. 1914-1920.

Newfoundland Quarterly

Andrews, T, Herd Well, Joe Kearney. Forgotten Heroes Magazine.
May. 1981.

Lacey, Amy. "From Arctic to Death." The Veteran Magazine. Sept.
1921.

DOCUMENTS

PANL. MG 562 Box 1. Logbooks of Legion of Frontiersmen at
Fort Waldegrave.

PANL. MG 632 Box 1. Minutes of Newfoundland Patriotic Association's monthly meetings.

PANL. MG 23. Information on the Royal Newfoundland Regiment. 1914-1918.

PANL. MG 438. World War I. Royal Newfoundland Regiment.

PANL. MG 439. World War I Documents.

PANL. MG 429.

PANL. GN 2/14.

PANL. GN 1/10. Royal Naval Reserve, Royal Newfoundland Regiment War correspondence.

PANL. GN 2/5. Newfoundland Royal Naval Reserve correspondence, 1902-1938.

PANL. GN 35/5 50th Anniversary-Royal Newfoundland Regiment,
correspondence, historical research, 1959-1964.

PANL. GN 2/14 F. A. 201.

PANL. GN 1/3/A File Newfoundland Patrol.

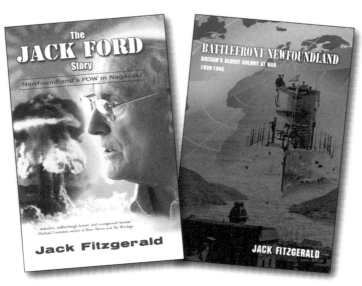